UNUSUAL
WINES

Pierrick Bourgault

JonGlez

Introduction

"How about a glass of wine?"

"Sorry, I don't know much about wine! I've always thought of taking a wine-tasting course, but it all seems so complicated ..."

We often hear this apologetic response, as if a skills assessment was needed before even taking a sip. The world of wine can often be intimidating and people worry about not being familiar with the jargon. They seem more comfortable savouring a chocolate or a beer. "The worst thing would be to take wine seriously: then you wouldn't want to drink it any more!" chuckles Michel Dovaz, a journalist who, at 87, tirelessly carries on his work as a wine taster and raconteur – the passion of a lifetime. Wine is human. It has a recognisable voice and face. This collection of traveller's tales pays homage to the winegrowers and winemakers who create wines to reflect their lands and their aspirations; and to the experts and merchants who distribute their wines to shops, restaurants and bistros.

I was lucky enough to experience three years of all-season work at the estates of Angélica Oury in Languedoc, Moselle and Champagne in France. I learned more from working in the vineyards, and listening to technical discussions and conversations with buyers, than I did training as an agricultural engineer. A big thank you to all!

To understand wine, all you need is common sense: grapes ripen faster in Spain than in Belgium; the higher the altitude, the cooler the climate; gravel retains less water than clay soil; if you let tea brew for a minute it won't have the same colour or taste as after an hour; alcohol acts as a preservative. Everything is logical, or at least there's an explanation relating to the history of the place or the people. Of course the multiplicity of labels, appellations and brands ranged along the shelves disorients the consumer, even if this diversity adds to its charm: "Wine is like a diamond: the more facets it has, the more beautiful it is. Without creativity, there's no identity!" as Camillo de Iuliis, the late owner of Farnese wines in the Abruzzo region of Italy, exclaimed. The wine landscape is vast and complex, which is why it's so interesting.

Harvest at Goriska Brda cooperative (Slovenia)

This guide is a blend of encounters and voices that recount both common and uncommon wine-producing techniques – all professionals, just like cooks, have their own secrets and tricks of the trade. There are classic methods for cultivating vines and making wine from the grapes, which our unusual examples irreverently contradict. The term "unusual" promises a different approach, a trip off piste with some extraordinary tales.

Beyond the intriguing explanations and entertaining anecdotes, this book aims to introduce the world of wine and the wines of the world.

My journey tells of the seasons and the viticulturists' activities throughout the year. It explains the various stages (planting, pruning, hoeing, harvesting, destemming, maceration, fermentation, bottling …) and their influence on the end product. Will you taste the local climate or *terroir* in the sensual magic of the wines? Think of Egyptian author Alaa Al Aswany's homage to wine in his novel *The Yacoubian Building*, which chronicles the life of a hedonistic Egyptian: "He learned the etiquette and rites of the royal bed chambers – the candles that burn all night, the glasses of French wine that kindle the flames of desire and obliterate fear …".

Today most areas of the world produce wines, just waiting for the curious to discover them. With open minds (and throats), let's taste the heritage of humanity, this timeless creation from the beginning of time.

When we taste a wine, our five senses are stimulated. Today's interactive age, although proud of its digital technology, is incapable of scanning a bottle and sending it via the internet; nor can it duplicate aromas and flavours or the emotion encapsulated in a glassful. Unlike movies or music, a bottle of wine cannot be reproduced. A glass of wine leaves a memory that we can only express in words to which everyone attaches their own meaning: "fruity", "sweet" and "soft" don't mean the same thing to all. This is a language to explore, to share, to put words into your mouth. In the word "oenology", *oenos* evokes wine, *logos* speech. The two are linked and wine loosens tongues.

Enjoy!

Contents

Uncommon climates 10
Taiwan's double harvests 16
Wines with altitude 20
Wines of Bali 24
Taiwanese ice wine. 28
Wines of the Gobi desert (China) 32
Quebec's ice wines 36

Off-the-radar *terroirs*. 40
Wine of Montmartre 44
A marine fossil *terroir* 48
Garage wines: amateur dramatics 50
Wine from non-grafted vines 54
The walled vines of the Azores 58
Wines of Pompeii 60
Wines of the Venetian lagoon 64

Amazing grapes 68
A monovarietal Bordeaux 74
A vine classified as a historic monument. 78
Vino della pace 82
Sinefinis: a political wine 86
Rare or forgotten varieties 88
Accursed, banned and mythical varieties 92
Wines from interplanted vines 96
PIWI grapes 100

Work in the vineyard **104**
   Vineyard music 110
   The *alberello* vines of Pantelleria (Italy) 116
   New Year's Eve harvests 120
   Vineyard horses 124
   Verjuice 130
   Biodynamic wine under the spotlight 134
   Wine from very old vines 140
   Jack and the beanstalk vines 144

Unconventional fermentation methods **148**
   Wines with little or no alcohol 154
   The strongest wine in the world 160
   Iraq's clandestine wines 164
   Rare sweet wines 170
   Wine that's really sulphite-free 174
   The amphora wines of Georgia 180
   Vegetarian wine 184
   Champagne, an English invention? 188
   Bordeaux made with dry ice 192
   A sparkling wine to disgorge at home 196

Curious colours **200**
   Greek rosé from the Oenoforos estate 204
   Pink champagne 208
   Yellow wine 212
   Orange wine 216
   Black wine 220

Extraordinary ageing methods **222**
   Underwater wine 228
   Ancient wines 232

Striking packaging **238**
   Odd bottles 242
   Original stoppers 246
   Labels with a difference 248
   Wooden labels 252

Uncommon climates

Life is a miracle. A balanced temperature, neither too hot nor too cold, throughout the seasons, with enough water to hydrate the plants but not so much that the roots would drown – either extreme could prove fatal.

Human intervention with the climate mainly involves irrigation. Without rainfall no plant can survive, but with abundant water the vigorous vine produces a vast canopy of stems and leaves among which the fruit fails to ripen properly. For such an invasive creeper to yield decent grapes for winemaking, ripe and intensely juicy at harvest time, neither too large nor gorged with water like those in the supermarket, it must receive the right amount of water.

Groundwater boreholes are the main source of irrigation. This technique is often criticised as it is water-intensive with high grape yields and dilute juice. Instead of drawing minerals from the depths of the soil, the roots just lie on the surface.

These methods that make it possible to grow grapes almost anywhere often produce wine without any local character. Logic suggests that vines should be planted where they can feed themselves, although Israeli engineers have developed a more economical system of drip-feeding through plastic pipes.

Moderate irrigation, however, gives the young vines time to take root; rainfall then supplies enough water for growth and maturity.

Frozen grapes in Quebec

In Mendoza (Argentina) the rainfall is enough for cacti but not for vines. For centuries the local peoples have channelled water from the Andes to the arid land at the foot of the mountains via an ingenious distribution network. The town of Mendoza resonates with streams rippling under the pavements, and in the countryside municipal employees maintain thousands of tiny channels. Market gardeners, horticulturists and viticulturists take turns to pay for a share of the water.

Cold is another threat to the vine, as it isn't a tree protected by thick bark but a creeper swollen with water. Although during winter it withstands temperatures as low as −15 °C, when the temperature falls still further the branches and trunks are permanently damaged. A spring frost of only −2° C harms the fragile buds and young leaves. The risk of crops being destroyed by cold prevents viticulture in northern latitudes or at high altitudes.

To extend these natural boundaries, however, generations of growers have come up with some ingenious solutions. Noting that cold air is heavier than warm air, they avoid planting vines at the bottom of a valley, where the temperature is lowest. They raise the vines off the ground by training them to grow higher, which slightly reduces the risk of frost damage.

Some techniques are costly as well as being environmentally unfriendly: heaters warm the air on frosty mornings; water is sprayed to cause a slight rise in temperature; fans, or even a helicopter flying overhead, stir up the cold air and replace it with the warm air from above … Winegrowers in Quebec even cover the vines with an insulating jacket.

Given enough water and sunshine, the vines will rampage over everything. This exuberant creeper, which is unable to stand upright, attaches its tendrils to whatever it can find and produces vast quantities of leaves, under the perplexed gaze of the winegrower, who'd rather see grapes. To limit this invasion of vegetation, the over-long stems must be pruned. In tropical climates, the vines are harvested two or three times a year.

In their book *The Magic of the 45th Parallel, the Ideal Latitude for the World's Great Wines*, Olivier Bernard and Thierry Dussard show that the 45th parallel – give or take 5° – is a climatically stable region where extreme temperatures cancel out: the climate is neither too hot nor too cold. The Singaporean Ch'ng Poh Tiong sees this parallel, equidistant between the North Pole and the equator, as the Buddha's Middle Way. But the region's incredible concentration of fine wines is also a reflection of history, and of course the effect of latitude is modified by altitude.

In the Southern Hemisphere the seasons are reversed. So it was to be expected that the first wine of the third millennium was made in South America by pressing the January 2000 harvest, while Europe had to wait until early October. For the same reason, Chinese technicians prefer to train in Australia (in March and April, during the grape harvest and winemaking) rather than in Europe, where the seasons of work in the vineyard are the same as at home.

Taiwan's double harvests

On this tropical island, two or three harvests a year give huge yields

"All seasons are good for growing grapes here," smiles Chen Ching Fung. "In France, you only have one!" The owner of a small theme park inspired by the world of wine, the Railway Valley Winery, he tells the story of the vineyard's year: "We cut back the vines in February–March, then the vine buds and leaves appear. We harvest in early July and immediately do a new cutback, leaving no green leaves on the stem. A second growing cycle begins, ending with a second harvest in November or December." For three annual cycles – and this practice concerns table grapes in particular – the vines will be cultivated under glass, even lit up at night, sometimes blitzed by irrigating them with salt water to stimulate fruiting. The only drawback of the climate is "typhoons that are more dangerous than insects and diseases", according to Hong Ji-Bei, grower at Tai Chung, in the centre west of the island on Shu Sheug estate. The vines aren't cultivated on trellises but on pergolas, which are more resistant to cyclones.

In Taiwan, the vineyards alternate with flooded rice fields and high-tech factories. On this island four times the size of Corsica, with a population density a hundred times greater, production is paramount. At about €500,000 a hectare, the land has to be as profitable as possible and the growers fertilise it heavily. Chang Shu-Gen, owner of the Song-He estate at Tai Chung, sprays three times: "potassium and nitrogen at pruning time and again when the grapes are half ripe; phosphorus before the harvest to harden the skins, discourage mildew and insect damage, together with animal waste, crushed seaweed and oysters." The winemakers even grow cabbages between the rows. Not a square metre is left bare.

Chen Ching Fung claims he produces 700 quintals of grapes per hectare (i.e. 7 kilos per square metre!) and some growers more than double that – ten times more than in Europe. The yields are so high that, even under the tropical climate, they have to add sugar before and after fermentation. "Because the customers like sweet wine," the grower justifies himself, choosing Japanese yeasts "to produce wine with the taste of oxidation and honey." Of course, Chen Ching Fung exports to Japan, the former colonising country. Particular attention is paid to the labels and the packaging: engraved glass and other personalised gifts for anniversaries, weddings, the birth of a child, a group of friends or military comrades … As in China, a bottle of wine is a prized gift.

The island also makes the most of its over-ripe fruit by distilling it, after fermentation, as "fruit wine". Of course the Taiwanese, who are curious travellers with a high standard of living, know the difference between these alcohols and the Western concept of wine developed from fermented grapes. The best European wines are sold in numerous stores.

Wines with altitude

What role does altitude play in climate and wine production? Where are the world's highest vineyards?

Every hiker wandering the mountains in summer knows that on leaving the baking heat of the valley, they'll need to don winter clothes a few hundred metres higher up, especially if they want to spend the night outside. Land that is suitable for a vineyard is defined by the nature of the soil, but also by the latitude – more or less northerly – and the altitude, which further lowers the temperature.

In France, logically enough, the highest vineyards are in the south. The vines of Irouléguy (Pyrénées-Atlantiques) grow at up to 450 metres. Given the steep slopes, part of the vineyard is planted on terraces that the mountains protect from the wind. The highest vineyards in France are in Savoie, planted 500 metres up in the microclimates of Ayze and Combe-de-Savoie. Also in Savoie, 700 metres above sea level and on a 60 per cent slope, a few heroic hectares are planted with local varieties: Mondeuse, Persan, Jacquère, Altesse ... Local features, such as the heat accumulated by a lake – Lake Geneva in Haute-Savoie – alleviate the winter temperatures. The climate of a place doesn't only depend on latitude or altitude. Warm ocean currents such as the Gulf Stream, the prevailing winds and the rotation of the Earth explain why the winter is significantly harsher in Quebec than in Burgundy, despite being at a similar latitude. Paradoxically, Burgundy is at a higher altitude.

Savoie

Not far from Savoie, Italy's Val d'Aosta claims to grow the highest vines in Europe, clinging to the foothills of Mont Blanc at up to 1,100 metres. The wines are known as *Enfer d'Arvier* and *Donnas* (reds), *La Salle* and *Morgex* (whites). Switzerland contends that, despite not being part of the European Union, it is in geographical Europe and has vineyards at a yet more remarkable altitude: 1,150 metres at Heidadorf-Visperterminen.

In the great scheme of things, these debates seem parochial. Towards the equator the climate becomes hot and humid and the vines produce grapes continuously, with over-watery juice according to the viticulturists, who prefer small, intensely flavoured grapes, skin rich in colour and aromas that transfer to the wine. At a given latitude, to benefit from a cooler climate, the solution is to plant a vineyard in the high-altitude soils of the mountainside. The highest French vineyards (1,200 metres) are at Cilaos on the island of Réunion in the Indian Ocean.

In Argentina, at 26° south latitude, the vineyard of Cafayate approaches 2,000 metres. Michel Rolland makes his *Yacochuya* wine from an old Malbec vine growing at 2,035 metres. The world's highest estate is thought to be Colomé (Argentina), where the vineyards rise in tiers from 2,300 to 3,111 metres among breathtaking scenery.

A negative altitude curiosity: the Loulan estate, in the "Turpan Depression" near the Gobi desert, lies at 150 metres below sea level (see p. 32).

The altitude of a vineyard, measured in metres, is indisputably an objective criterion, but it begs the question of whether we are referring to vines growing at an exceptional altitude where the grapes ripen unevenly, or at a lower level where they give consistent quality at an acceptable cost in labour.

Wines of Bali

**These wines are original in three ways:
for the tropical climate of the island, the grape varieties
and Indonesia's Islamic tax system**

In Bali, latitude 8° south, the temperature is warm all year round: 27 °C on average. The humidity varies according to the season, dry or wet, but remains high; tropical vegetation grows without a winter break. An unusual climate for the vine, which is a Mediterranean plant accustomed to a more frugal diet. Humidity causes disease (downy mildew, powdery mildew ...) but the main risk is producing an abundance of large grapes with dilute juice, without the intense flavour needed for quality winemaking.

Another feature of this island is that despite the religion being Hinduism it uses the tax system of Indonesia, the world's most populous Muslim country, and wine imports are heavily taxed. Around 1992, Ida Bagus Rai Budarsa, heir to a family of rice wine producers and holder of an invaluable distribution licence, determined to avoid these taxes on imports by making wine on the island. The Indonesian investor joined forces with French oenologist Vincent Desplat and they tried to ferment the only available grapes, the local red table variety Alphonse-Lavallée, which the local farmers grow to eat and to make offerings to their Hindu gods.

In 1994 the Hatten estate, property of Ida Bagus Rai Budarsa, launched a fresh and fruity rosé wine that was well suited to the island's spicy maritime cuisine. Every week throughout the year, the company buys grapes locally, presses them and makes wine. Trade visitors are always surprised by the small size of the press, in relation to the estate's output – 1.5 million litres per year. In temperate climates, the equipment is of course used only once a year, at the harvest season, so has to be on a larger scale.

Once the grape harvest is over in Bali, the vines are pruned and then rebud, putting out new leaves, flowers and grapes that are harvested four months later (the year has 2.8 growing cycles). The estate now cultivates 35 hectares of a mysterious variety of white grape, Belgia Muscat, while continuing to buy red grapes from the farmers. The vines, supported by pergolas (arbours), are high yielding and the workers are simultaneously protected from the sun. They've found the perfect solution.

Twenty years of astonishingly hard work seem to have paid off: winemaking is indeed possible in the tropics. A red, two whites and two sparkling wines (traditional champagne method) complete the range. Hatten also imports frozen blocks of unfermented grape juice from Australia, including the skin and seeds – no alcohol, so no taxes – and turns them into wine in Bali under the *Two Islands* label.

Another unusual speciality: Maryse La Rocque from Quebec, the estate's marketing officer who appreciates the famous sweet aperitif *Pineau des Charentes*, has launched a vintage of the same type.

Finally, an amusing paradox: this winery thrives thanks to the Islamic anti-alcohol taxation. The island's hotel chains (Hyatt, Novotel, Four Seasons, Aman ...) find it difficult to import bottles from the rest of the world to cater for their wine-loving guests, so they buy from the one and only estate on the island that uses local grapes. Hatten doesn't export its wines. For a tasting session, you'll have to visit Bali.

Taiwanese ice wine

Ice wine or iced wine?

Not just anyone can produce ice wine. Especially in a tropical country such as Taiwan. According to Resolution 6/2003 of the International Organisation of Vine and Wine (www.oiv.int), this speciality is defined as "Wine made exclusively from the fermentation of fresh grapes having undergone cryoselection in the vineyard without recourse to physical procedures". The grapes selected to produce ice wine are harvested frozen and pressed in this state, at a recommended temperature lower or equal to −7 °C, when the water and sugar separate.

The geopolitical situation of Taiwan is curious: the United Nations has never acknowledged this democracy coveted by China, which the World Health Organization even considers a "Chinese province". Taiwan isn't a member of the OIV and doesn't follow its rules, which is why the so-called ice wines from some Taiwanese producers are made from chilled, not frozen, grapes.

At Tai Chung in the centre-west of the island, at the Shu Sheug estate, self-taught winemaker Hong Ji-Bei keeps grapes in cold storage at 1 °C for a month before pressing, so that they dry out and concentrate in flavour. This wine, with its significant sugar residues and jam flavours, is served in the tiny glasses used for rice wine.

In his Railway Valley Winery, Chen Ching Fung prepares ice wine on the same principle. It is sold on site in a room open to locals and Chinese tourists. To meet new clients and advertise their range, Hong Ji-Bei and his son organise tasting sessions for their dry or sweet wines.

Another violation of the rules of ice wine: cane sugar presumably sweetens the grape juice and wine. During a visit to Chang Shu-Gen at the Song He estate, the sight of bags of sugar piled up in the cellar inspired this remark: "The customers like sweet wine, so I add sugar after fermentation." Of course there is nothing toxic in this additive, necessary because the tropical vines yield huge amounts of unripe grapes.

True ice wine, produced according to OIV good practice in Germany, Austria, Alsace and Quebec, is rich in natural grape sugars but especially in the aroma of candied fruits and honey – the desired result.

Whether the raisins are for jam, the table or the winemaking vat seems to make little difference to these self-taught winemakers. Many of them have learned their craft from a viticulture treatise by the former Japanese colonists.

"In 1963, my father gave me this book that taught me everything," says Hong Ji-Bei. "I was 14 when my enthusiasm for vines and wines began."

Chen Ching Fung and his Railway Valley Winery

Wines of the Gobi desert (China)

How can wine be made in a land frozen in winter, torrid in summer and with never a drop of rain?

Nothing predisposes western China, on the Mongolian border, to the cultivation of vines. Over 2,500 kilometres from the sea, this is the most continental region in the world: in winter, with temperatures between −20 °C and −30 °C, plants completely freeze.

These obstacles weren't enough to deter the Chinese: in 1949, when Peking annexed Turkestan, which is two and a half times the size of France, an ancient irrigation system brought water from the Tian Shan mountains to the oases of the Silk Road. The Uighurs had cultivated vines for centuries to produce raisins.

So Peking named this region Xinjiang (New Frontier) and from 1980 decided to plant thousands of hectares with Western grape varieties (Cabernet Sauvignon, Syrah, Merlot, Chardonnay, Chenin Blanc, Riesling …) as well as local varieties (Beichun, Cibayi, Shabulawe …). In eastern China, the land in provinces such as Shandong is expensive, criss-crossed with road networks and conurbations, and polluted by industry.

Plain after earthing-up

Citic Guo'An wineries

So that vines will flourish in the former desert, the ditches between the rows are flooded six to ten times a year. "Here, no rain, so no diseases, treatments, copper, or sulphur!" assures Grégory Michel, who runs part of the Loulan estate organically. These 90 hectares, an area similar to the largest European vineyards, produce an amazing local Muscat, *Rou Ding Xiang*, which is naturally sweet when fermented and popular with the Japanese. Their top-of-the-range wines, packaged like precious perfumes, sell for €150 a bottle.

But how to protect the rootstock from frost? On winter evenings, the market gardeners of Xinjiang cover their greenhouses with thick quilting; or sometimes blankets packed around the vines does the trick. In the Gobi desert, as soon as the September harvest is over, the farmers and migrant workers waste no time in pruning the vines, bending over the stems and burying them in furrows that they protect by covering with soil. By late October, the earthing-up has erased all sign of vegetation from the landscape. Over tens of thousands of hectares, there is just the plain bristling with bare stakes (see photo p. 33). In spring, the plentiful labour force arrives to unearth the vines, tie them up again and regrowth begins – always with the risk of a late frost.

On its 10,000 hectares, Citic Guo'An wineries produce a rosé from the Syrah grape, *Suntime Yili River*, which you can sample at the Restaurant du Monde Autogrill at the Carrousel du Louvre (Paris) for €12 per bottle. Paradoxically, this Chinese wine isn't sold in China because, as confirmed by Yiran Liu, director of the Maison du Languedoc-Roussillon in Shanghai, "The Chinese market isn't ready for rosé. Men don't order it because they consider it a women's drink." Citic Guo'An has also created a Riesling-based *Sushi Time* wine to accompany Japanese restaurant specialities, which is also exported.

Quebec's ice wines

Intrepid winemakers succeed in this glacial climate

Since the discovery of the territory by French explorer Jacques Cartier in 1534, viticulture in Quebec has experienced many setbacks. Although Montreal is at the same latitude as the Bordeaux vineyards and Quebec is on a level with Burgundy, the climatic conditions are harsher. Winter kills the vine stocks if they aren't protected, frosts threaten the spring buds, the too-short summer makes it difficult for the vine to complete its growth cycle and the autumn snow follows close behind the grape pickers.

The first rootstock imported for communion wine froze, and when the vines did survive the grapes failed to ripen. In the late 19th century, some growers were planting hardier varieties. Quebec escaped a total alcohol ban in the Prohibition era, but cheap imports competed with local production and after 1930 there were no vineyards left. After four centuries of failure, it seemed an impossible dream, just as Cartier was convinced he'd found gold and diamonds in Asia when in fact he'd taken on board the pyrite and quartz of North America.

But winemakers love a challenge. Planting resumed around 1980 with grape varieties suited to the climate such as Seyval, Vidal, Geisenheim, Cayuga, Éona (whites) and Maréchal Foch, Sainte-Croix, Chaunac, Chancellor (reds). As vigorous as they were fast-growing, these varieties managed to complete their growth cycle in record time. To withstand the cold of winter, the stems are banked up (covered with a pile of soil in early November, which is removed in late April or early May) using a tractor and special tools. The growers have the most incredible equipment: burners to warm the vines, fans to combat the spring frosts, helicopters to push warm air towards the ground. Snow cannon have even been used to provide a white coat protecting the ground from the polar temperatures.

Most amazing of all, though, is the ice wine made from a grape harvest in December or January at temperatures of −8 °C to −12 °C. As water freezes at 0 °C, the ice crystals remain in the press which is kept at −7 °C: a phenomenon known as cryoselection. The concentrated juice extracted is higher in sugars and acidity and hence in aroma than it would be if the grapes were harvested and pressed at warmer temperatures. Quebec therefore respects the International Organisation of Vine and Wine rules on true ice wine.

Although 100 kilos of grapes normally yield 80–85 litres of juice, the volume is only 12–15 litres in these extreme temperatures. Working in freezing conditions for such a small yield means that ice wine is an exclusive and expensive speciality: a 0.20 litre bottle sells for around €20. Tasting reveals aromas of apricot, mango, honey and candied fruit, with a lovely fresh finish.

There are only around a dozen producers of ice wine in Quebec.

Off-the-radar *terroirs*

Terroir is the French buzzword for the characteristics of a winegrowing region, including climate, soil and exposure to the elements. It suggests back-breaking toil and a sense of place – both the myth of a promised land and ancient land divisions. In my early days of reporting from Uruguay, a viticulturist confided his life's goal: "To make a wine like Uruguay." I had noted and quoted that charming phrase, which probably cropped up during every guided tour of the estate. A few weeks later, in Italy, I heard exactly the same remark from another owner, hand on heart: "I want to produce a wine like Sicily!"

But *terroir* is not only marketing hype, a poetic invention for the vague inaccuracy of labels. Nobody would claim that the waters of Volvic and Evian are the same – the minerality of the soil also plays a role in wine, which is about 85 per cent water. How does the soil hold the rainwater to feed the roots? Can the roots reach the water table? What minerals do the vines obtain from the soil?

When you arrive at an estate, examine the ground and the stone walls of the houses. In Piedmont, a winegrower from the village of Monferrato – which was an independent state for centuries – called out to me, while pointing at the castle walls: "Don't move, just look around you: these walls show the type of soil. Limestone can hold water." The very first step, before you've seen or drunk anything, is to observe the cellar walls and the stones along the path and imagine what type of wine will be produced.

Vines grown at Pompeii by Mastroberardino

A windswept valley is less humid; the clusters of grapes dry faster after rain or morning dew, and so are less susceptible to disease. Between the northern and southern slopes of the same hill, the average temperature varies several degrees: architects and builders are well aware of this. Is the prevailing wind warm or cold? Does it bring maritime humidity or desert aridity? This changes everything. Some Greek viticulturists look for plots that face north, or lie at a high altitude, which means that the grapes will ripen more slowly. The *terroir* dramatically affects the climate: in the tropics, it's enough to climb a few thousand metres to find a mountain climate and cool nights.

The modern scientific concept of *terroir* covers more than the soil type and local climate and includes local know-how, typical native yeasts, and historical precedents used to define the *appellation d'origine* system.* By taking into account the local climate, soil type, grape variety, traditions, micro-organisms and history, character traits emerge in a coherent whole. The legal designation of origin is an identity in a given geographical area, a collective label that belongs to all those who wish to recognise it. Does the wine reflect the winemaker or is it a reflection of the *terroir*? To what extent does human creativity come into play?

The fact that a vineyard exists in a particular place is due to a combination of natural and historical circumstances. On the shores of Lake Geneva, for example, the vines benefit from three sources of warmth: the sun, its reflection on the surface of the water, and the heat given off at night by the rocks. These "three suns" help the vines to survive a cold climate and a high altitude. The presence of water creates a a microclimate, because of thermal inertia that evens out temperature fluctuations. Formerly, waterways such as the Garonne and the Rhone were the only practical routes for transporting wine, so the great French vineyards were planted alongside them. The railway lines later played the same role.

Unusual *terroirs* include Parisian vineyards, suburban garages, the rootstock of the historic site of Pompeii, the rediscovered wine of the Venetian lagoon, and the UNESCO-listed viticultures of the Italian island of Pantelleria and Pico Island in the Azores.

*Appellation d'Origine Protégée/Contrôlée (AOP/AOC) are the French terms for wines of a Protected Designation of Origin (PDO); an EU system of designating (and protecting) regions and areas for wine production.

Wine of Montmartre

City-centre wine
Reminder of a time when Île-de-France was the country's largest and most prosperous wine-producing region

Around the 2nd and 3rd centuries AD, the Parisii were so fond of the wines of Italy and southern Gaul that they planted vines in their good city of Lutetia. It's true that the grapes didn't ripen properly in the local climate but the slightly acidic flavours were greatly appreciated and the calcareous soil turned out to be suitable for a vineyard. The royal city was rich and workshops making amphorae and winepresses proliferated, as archaeological digs have revealed. Around the Parisian abbeys the monks planted vines, harvested grapes and made wine with the same enthusiasm as they did in Burgundy.

Alain Valentin, the great troubadour of the Commanderie de Montmartre, tells the story of this *king of wines and wine of kings*: "That of the Goutte d'Or was the favourite of King Louis IX (better known as Saint-Louis, 1214–1270). On every anniversary of the royal coronation, the City of Paris was in the habit of offering four *muids** of this precious nectar to the palace." In the 18th century, over 40,000 hectares of vines fuelled the unquenchable thirst of a prosperous and densely populated region.

But as quality doesn't necessarily go with quantity, the high yields of unripe grapes gave an acidic wine known as *guinguet* (etymology unknown) "that could make goats dance, but people lapped it up", continues Valentin. With its low alcohol content, *guinguet* didn't keep well and would turn to vinegar if not quickly drunk in the *guinguettes*, the ubiquitous popular cabaret and dance halls.

In the 19th century the railways brought better-quality, cheaper wines from the south of France, the expansion of Paris increased the cost of land, phylloxera killed off the rootstock and during the First World War the winemakers were slaughtered too. In the space of half a century, 2,000 years of local production were snuffed out.

*In Paris a *muid* was equivalent to 268,220 litres (8 cubic feet).

In 1933, however, the City of Paris planted the tiny vineyard of Montmartre because the resident artists had objected to a building project in a garden on the northern slopes of the hill. So a vine grew in memory of those that had covered the sunnier southern slopes. Traditional harvests and vintages were sponsored by well-known artists: Mistinguett, Fernandel, Annie Cordy, Maxime Le Forestier, Pierre Perret, Gérard Jugnot, Laurent Voulzy, Nagui, Hélène Ségara, Anne Roumanoff … Growing among the 1,800 almost exclusively red grapes (75 per cent Gamay, 20 per cent Pinot Noir, Seibel and Merlot) are a few Sauvignon Blanc, Gewurztraminer and Riesling varieties. The 18th *arrondissement* town hall is the only one in France whose cellar contains a bottling plant. Declaration of harvesting and bottling, tax paid, all above board.

Le Clos Montmartre is now sold during the harvest festival and throughout the year at the Tourist Office for municipal social events – while stocks last. Some old bottles are "undrinkable", as the Festival Committee website announces with commendable frankness. Since a winemaker has become involved, however, the quality has improved significantly.

Festive harvest of Bistrot Mélac's two vines, Paris, 11th arrondissement

Other Parisian wines

Vineyards are now being revived in Paris: vines can be found growing at Saint-Germain-des-Prés, in Square Félix-Desruelles; in the private garden of Saint-François-Xavier church presbytery; in Parc de Bercy (the site of vast wine warehouses, between Gare d'Austerlitz and Gare de Lyon) and Parc Georges-Brassens; in a mansion garden at Parc de Bagatelle in the Bois de Boulogne; at Montmartre; on Butte Bergeyre, rue Georges Lardennois;

in the middle of Parc de Belleville; at Suresnes, in the Clos du Pas Saint-Maurice; and at Neuilly-Plaisance in the garden of Pierre Facon. Other planters prefer to remain anonymous.

According to Patrice Bersac, the president of Vignerons Franciliens Réunis, the Île-de-France region has over 200 vineyards spread over some 20 hectares and produces 100,000 bottles of wine a year.

In mid-September (on a Saturday), the two vines at Bistrot Mélac are triumphantly harvested in a festive atmosphere. Oenologists diligently measure the sugar level in the fermenting juice that produces around thirty bottles of *Château Charonne* – a fantastic harvest from only two vines.

The only golden rule is that without "plantation rights", any vineyard that produces grapes for winemaking is illegal, whatever the area or the number of vines. Any fermented grape produce is subject to strict winemaking regulations, both European and French. Some local customs offices impose fines, or have the bottled wine and the vines destroyed, while others turn a blind eye. At present, Vignerons Franciliens Réunis are trying to secure recognition for "heritage, experimental, educational, historic, cultural" vines and an "academy of heritage and biodiversity".

Bird netting on Pierre Facon's vines at Neuilly-Plaisance

A marine fossil *terroir*

The vines and wines of *Château Coquillas* evoke the role of *terroir* and its past incarnations

In the Pessac-Léognan appellation zone of Bordeaux, the Château de France vineyard extends over the highest of the four terraces, where the soil is composed of jasper, flint, lydian "touchstone", quartz and quartzite in browns, whites, reds and pinks. The *Château Coquillas* label, with its mineral notes, comes from vines rooted in a remarkable layer of marine fossils.

This soil, which is truly an open-air geological and palaeontological museum, bears witness to the changing course of the Garonne since the end of the Tertiary and during the Quaternary. As the glacial episodes came and went, the river deposited pebbles mixed with clay, sand, hardpan, limestone and other faluns (hardpan is a dense layer of compressed sand and gravel; faluns are fossils in marine limestone) – the constituent elements of the Bordeaux Graves (gravels) region. The growers appreciate the fact that the soil retains the heat of the day and releases it during the night.

So the roots of the *Château Coquillas* vines penetrate the remains of turret shells, bivalves and other molluscs dating from the formation of the land.

The wine label's shell motif is a visual illustration of the concept of *terroir* and the importance of rooting: 2–5 metres deep in the case of young vines, but the roots can plunge down as far as 15 metres. This link to the land becomes much closer when all the secondary roots, rootlets and absorbent hairs are taken into account. Together they cover astonishing distances: 300,000 kilometres for an average tree, according to ethnobotanist Pierre Lieutaghi. Symbolically, the roots and the earth evoke the world of the dead, the invisible forces. The *terroir* is much more than just a poetic image.

> A strange paradox: this stony soil, where only vines can thrive and which is unsuitable for agriculture, is now much more valuable than arable land.

Other marine fossils at Astéries in the Entre-Deux-Mers region
To investigate the subsoil into which the plant plunges secretly and invisibly, take along your pickaxe or simply observe the pebbles lying on the ground, look into any ditches and examine the walls of old buildings nearby. For example, the limestone at Astéries in the Entre-Deux-Mers region of Aquitaine (France), also known as Bordeaux stone or Saint-Émilion limestone, dates from the lower Oligocene (32 million years ago). The name comes from the innumerable Asterias sea stars (a type of starfish) and other marine fossils, oysters and corals found in the soil.

Garage wines: amateur dramatics

"The government built us houses with garages, but we had no cars! So we made wine!"

In rural France before 1980, it was common to press your own fruit for cider or wine, depending on the region, and happily distil the juice.

The grapes were not always ripe when harvested and were macerated with their stems;* this yielded a must that was something between grape juice and vinegar. The bouquet was sometimes baffling.

The wines were both good and bad, among the best and the worst. Winemaking is an art. In France, legislation and customs duties have made things so complex from the administrative point of view that home winemaking has almost died out. The aim was to avoid excess and to professionalise the quality of the product, but sadly the great diversity and sense of initiative have been lost.

In Italy, winemaking is still alive and well. In Georgia, some locals are proud to offer you their "house wine". Slovenian winemakers will laughingly tell how they started up: "After the 1976 earthquake, the government built us houses with garages ... but we had no cars! So we made wine!"

The expression "garage wine" also covers a *cuvée confidentielle* of only around several hundred bottles from a great winemaker.

*The green woody stems make the wine taste astringent, with an unpleasant bitterness, if macerated with the fruit, so the stems are usually removed with a mechanical destemmer, or by hand a cluster at a time.

How to become an amateur winemaker

Itsmywine.com helps you choose from among fifteen varieties selected throughout France by Olivier Magny and Nicolas Paradis, founders of the Parisian wine bar Ô Chateau, to create a blend that will be delivered to you in bottles with your own label.

Many sites such as www.mabouteille.fr sell personalised cases and labels. Others, such as www.unpiedaudomaine.com, let you accompany a winemaker during the growing and harvesting seasons, sponsor a vine, and help with the pruning, the grape harvest and various stages of vinification. The "co-winemaker" can then "co-sign" the wine.

Another way of linking up with a winegrower is through crowdfunding or participatory financing: professionals seeking extra funds for an investment (such as a plough or vats …) subscribe to www.fundovino.com and participants are acknowledged in kind, usually with bottles of wine.

You can also meet amateur winemakers, who are often happy to share the tricks of the trade with beginners: they will explain how to make a press from a truck jack, convert an old freezer to separate tartaric acid, use a diabetic urine test to measure sugar levels, or a tank recycled from a dairy farm for thermovinification …

Michel Rouzière, amateur winemaker at Saint-Fraimbault-de-Prières (Mayenne), using a destemmer

An example of garage wine: the "Cuvée des amis" at Mayenne (France)

Ever-original garage wine begins with a new vine plantation or with an existing variety. In the apple-growing region of northern Mayenne, Michel Rouzière was successfully making cider. So why not make some wine? He asked around: in the 19th century, his village of Saint-Fraimbault-de-Prières produced its own wine. A friend from Maine-et-Loire brought Cabernet Franc (red) and Chenin (white) rootstock that Rouzière planted near his home. He recycled equipment and embarked on a steep technical learning curve. To choose the best time for the harvest, for example, he examines the grape juice with a refractometer, an optical device that measures the concentration of sugar. A hydrometer shows the amount of sugar in the must – and thus the alcohol potential. "I just have to add 1.25 kilos of sugar to reach a density of 1090 and an alcohol content of 12.50 per cent," he calculates. "The acidity of the Cabernet will be assessed and adjusted with potassium bicarbonate when the fermentation is complete." Rouzière took early retirement and expanded, acquiring an abandoned plot in the Sarthe planted with Pineau d'Aunis, Gamay and Cabernet Franc. He then approached local restaurants to see if they would buy his wine.

Once you've heard this passionate winemaker's stories, there remains the tasting experience. Will the result live up to expectations? In 2014 we tasted his *Cuvée des amis* 2011 red. Visually, this three-year-old wine still displays beautiful purple highlights. No oxidation or premature changes, a clean job. To the nose, no faults, serene aromas. On tasting, agreeably fruity, fresh, fine tannins and a long finish. And the miracle happens: you forget Rouzière's garage, his tiny destemmer and toy winepress, plastic dog-food containers (spotlessly clean) for collecting the grapes, the label designed on his daughter's computer … We tasted a wine that could have come from a professional estate to find its place on the shelves of a wine merchant or the menu of a good restaurant.

Wine from non-grafted vines

A few own-root vines thrive in the rare *terroirs* free of phylloxera

Around 1860, an aphid-like insect attacked the roots of European grapevines (*Vitis vinifera* species), sapping their strength and killing them within two or three years. This parasite from America advanced at around 30 kilometres a year and destroyed the viticulture of entire regions: only sandy or volcanic soils were spared as they stop the insect settling around the roots of the vine.

As there was no question of replanting all the vineyards in sand or volcanic terrain and even the most aggressive chemical treatments had failed, a solution was found in 1870 with the introduction of biodiversity. The current debate between supporters of chemical and biological methods is nothing new …

Scientists had observed that the rootstock of American vines (such as *Vitis labrusca*, *Vitis riparia* and *Vitis aestivalis*) was resistant to the parasite, but unfortunately their grapes proved disappointing to winemakers. There were two ways round this: crossing American and European vines to obtain "hybrid direct producers" with the qualities of both parents, or planting resistant American rootstock and grafting on a European variety.

Own-root vine from the pre-phylloxera era at Sarragachies (Gers, France)

Non-grafted rootstock, Xinjiang (China)

Young grafted vines ready for planting (Italy)

Over thirty years, almost all Europe's diseased vineyards were renewed in this way. Some vines that were growing in sandy or volcanic soil before 1860 nevertheless resisted the parasite: they are referred to as "own-root" varieties. France has some of these survivors from the pre-phylloxera era: the vine of Sarragachies, listed on the Inventory of Historic Monuments in 2012 (see p. 78); three plots in Champagne (Chaudes-Terres, Clos Saint-Jacques and Croix-Rouge) vinified by Bollinger under the name *Vieilles vignes françaises*, which produce under 4,000 bottles a year, sold at over €400 the bottle; and a plot of own-root Tannat grape planted in 1871 that in 2012 yielded the special vintage *Vignes pré-phylloxériques* from Plaimont Producteurs – only 1,000 bottles at over €50, numbered and reserved in advance. Outside France, own-root vines can be found in Brazil (where part of the wine grape varieties are *Vitis* but not *vinifera*), on the volcanic island of Santorini in Greece, in Italy close to Vesuvius and Etna, and in the desert sands of Xinjiang (China).

Another quality of this type of vine is used by Chinese winemakers to keep the stems flexible, so that they can be bent into the irrigation ditches and covered with earth in autumn. They are divided when they become too woody and rigid. Of course, in the previous year's pruning, the grower will have chosen the young and vigorous replacement shoots as "life insurance". This technique gives sprightly vines that are easily bent, nourished by the ancient strong roots and firmly anchored in the minerals of the *terroir*. The vines of Xinjiang, including those of Guoanwine, are managed on this principle to produce a rosé called *Suntime Yili River*. It bears no comparison with wines from the primordial plots of Plaimont or Bollinger in France, although it also comes from own-root vines.

The walled vines of the Azores

Volcanic soil for vines inscribed on UNESCO's World Heritage List

Although this Portuguese archipelago in the Atlantic, 1,500 kilometres from Europe, is now more famous for its high atmospheric pressure (Azores High) than for its wine, the islanders have managed to get the best out of the small amount of cultivable land in the volcanic mountainous terrain by planting vines. To protect the vines from the sea breeze and salt spray, they excavated the lava and covered the landscape with tiny fields surrounded by dark basalt walls. These more or less regularly shaped *currais* or *curraletas*, as they're called, each enclose a dozen or so vines and create an extraordinary landscape inscribed as a UNESCO World Heritage site.

Grants are even provided for their maintenance, which is very labour-intensive and costly. The dark stone plays its part by storing heat during the day and releasing it at night, creating a unique microclimate.

In this distinctive *terroir*, the grapes mature quickly, ripening and drying on the vine. There's no need to tie them up or raisin them in dryers in order to obtain straw wine. Before the grapes dry out, the winemakers pick and press the clusters to obtain very sweet juices, which mature into sweet wines. These wines have long been exported to make the island's fortune: the noblest tables in Europe, even the Russian tsars, appreciated the Verdelho dessert wine of Pico Island.

Around 1850, oidium (powdery mildew) attacked the Azores. This fungal disease from America is caused by a white micro-organism. The vines withered and in the subsequent economic disaster people began to emigrate.

There are, however, chemical or biological solutions: sulphur spray, developed in the Languedoc in 1856 by Henri Marès, or the adoption of American vines that are resistant to the persistent enemy. Thus the Isabella red grape variety was planted in the Azores before the disease could be brought under control.

Today, Terceira Island produces a sweet wine named Biscoitos after the planting holes dug into the lava, which are round like biscuits.

Local labels are *Verdelho des Açores* and *Terrantez*. *Lajido* is a sweet white from Pico Island. The hybrid grape Noah, which has long been banned in France (see p. 92 on banned varieties) is fermented for local consumption.

Wines of Pompeii

Two thousand years after the tragedy, Pompeii's vines reveal ancient techniques

On 24 August in the year AD 79, there was a devastating eruption of Vesuvius. The delightful coastal town of Pompeii and the vineyards that had supplied the appreciative court of Rome were all preserved under the solidified ash. A longstanding viticultural tradition had been inherited from the Greeks; the frescoes unearthed by archaeologists show the importance accorded to the vines growing on the slopes of the volcano. The plain was used to grow food because, according to the Roman proverb, "Bacchus loves the hills." Vines, roots and stakes moulded in the ash have been excavated. These remarkable finds reveal the vine-training methods of the ancient world: the planting frame was 4 Roman feet square (1.18 x 1.18 metres) for vines worked by hand, larger for those where draft animals passed – as Pliny the Elder's *Historia Naturalis* (*Natural History*) confirms.

As land was scarce in the urban area, the Pompeian owners looked for high yields. Planted in tight rows on the rich basalt soil, the vines provided dense vegetation and their shade kept down the weeds and hence the labour of removing them. So the vines had the soil's entire mineral and water reserves to themselves. The workers benefited from the shade too. The high pergolas (trellising) protected the grapes from ground predators, and the leaf canopy offered protection from the beady eyes of birds. These ingenious Romans optimised the yields of both labour and land.

The pergola wasn't the only vine-training system practised in antiquity. Pliny the Elder and the agronomist Columella cite five others: "coverage", with stems laid on the ground, as in the cultivation of melons; the free-standing *gobelet* or bush **vine system**; the "spindle" vertical cordon on trellising; the "curtain" horizontal cordon supported by stakes, with a straight branch replacing the wire of trellised vines; and *alberate,* growing like a wild vine on a living tree, as still found near Naples with the Asprinio grape. The Romans, excellent winemakers that they were, adapted their vine training to different climates and *terroirs*. These six methods of cultivation can be seen in the vineyard of the Gallo-Roman Saint-Romain-en-Gal museum in Vienne (France). During the tragedy of Pompeii, Pliny became a victim of his own scientific curiosity, overcome by Vesuvius' sulphurous fumes.

Today, in the heart of the historic city, the Mastroberardino estate has planted 1.5 hectares with the local red varieties Piedirosso, Aglianico and Sciascinoso, close to the antiquities described by Pliny and depicted in frescoes. The only concessions to our age are that the plants are grafted onto American rootstock for fear of phylloxera. Pergola cultivation has been partially replaced by poles, trellising or free-standing bushes so that the grapes ripen better.

The wine is made using modern methods. "Otherwise it would be too rough to drink!" smiles the oenologist. The aim is twofold: to understand the old techniques and to disseminate the history of winemaking in the Campania region.

A bottle of *Villa dei misteri* (Villa of the Mysteries) red retails for about €100.

This is all a reminder that every vineyard is a cultural research field and wine is our common heritage.

Wines of the Venetian lagoon

A salty *terroir* by the sea

Before Michel Thoulouze settled in Venice, he had launched television channels such as Planète, Canal Jimmy, CinéCinéma and Seasons. How has this audiovisual producer become a wine producer? "I like to create things, change the landscape, starting from scratch. I'd never have bought an existing estate. My hobby has become my profession."

The island of Sant'Erasmo is part of the municipality of Venice, but bears no resemblance to the city visited every year by 20 million tourists. When Thoulouze discovered some abandoned gardens by the sea, he consulted his winegrowing friends in Burgundy, who told him: "Venice is an excellent marketing idea, but the wine must be good …" But vines don't like salt.

Thoulouze settled there on a hunch. He came across a 17th-century map showing the location of a vineyard on his land. "Soil analysis revealed traces of copper, meaning there must have been vines growing that were later abandoned, everything here being so difficult."

This man didn't shrink from the difficulties – on the contrary. On the advice of Claude Bourguignon, a bioagriculturalist, he chose not to plough but to sow barley, Chinese radishes and sorghum for four years to prepare the soil. "The neighbours were telling us we were crazy to plant vines without working the soil." Next, with oenologist Alain Graillot of Crozes-Hermitage, he chose "old white varieties that could have been planted at the time of the Venetian Republic: Istrian Malvasia, Vermentino and Fiano d'Avellino."

Another unusual choice was to use own-root plants – i.e. not grafted onto American rootstock that is resistant to phylloxera – betting on the fact that the salinity would mitigate the aggressiveness of the parasite.

Why take the risk of planting own-root vines? "To recover the original taste of the wine," says Thoulouze. "The ungrafted plant is weird, it produces fewer grapes, some are large and others small, they grow like a bunch of adolescents, not all at the same rate. In the end, the wine is much better than expected. It hasn't much aroma but it's got plenty of body. Drink one glass and you want another. My wine is called *Orto*, which means garden, orchard."

Bottling is done on a truck that arrives by boat – in Venice nothing is simple. Thoulouze gets around on an Ape (Italian for bee), the light three-wheeled vehicle that doesn't compact the soil, and he delivers by boat. His 4.5 hectares currently produce 10,000 bottles, soon to rise to 20,000. The mayor of Venice buys bottles as gifts for the city's guests.

As one of the neighbouring farmers says: "This is the first time a wine of ours has been labelled!" Michel Thoulouze has earned the respect of his neighbours by his simple determination and, as he points out, "the Italians have a culture of immigration".

Amazing grapes

The history of the different varieties of grape is as long as the vine itself. This invasive creeper, which, unlike a tree, is unable to support itself, attaches itself to neighbouring plants and gradually spreads to conquer new ground. Extremes of climate kill off the most fragile plants and, year after year, the most resistant are selected.

Every year, sexual reproduction between the male and female flowers produces a grape whose seeds contain a genetic heritage that is slightly different to its parentage and sometimes better adapted to local conditions. Predators, especially birds, crunch the sweet grapes and inadvertently sow their seeds. The stems fall to the ground and take root in their turn: a natural phenomenon known as layering. These two methods of propagation – sexual and asexual – give rise to huge biological diversity.

When people first began to take an interest in a particular vine, they uprooted and replanted it, waiting to see whether it would thrive. Using the layering technique, a piece of stem was planted in the soil so that new roots would grow there. Plant surgery was also attempted by grafting the tissues of one vine onto a different rootstock. Finally, people left their mark on the land by choosing the varieties best suited to the local climate: those that bud after the last spring frosts and ripen before the changeable autumn weather.

This slow evolution of plant populations is characteristic of the genetic identity of the land: in this way, local varieties that are naturally adapted to their environment are created and developed.

A grape *variety* refers to a group of consistent appearance, equivalent to a *breed* of animals. Here are a few definitions:

Table varieties are intended for eating. One example is the Italia grape with its large crunchy berries, cultivated in Sicily in vast rows of polytunnels and harvested from May onwards. Some seedless varieties are popular, particularly when dried as raisins.

Vat varieties are for winemaking: as their berries are smaller than table grapes, the higher proportion of skin brings flavour and colour to the wine. They always have seeds, which contribute greatly to the taste.

Some table grapes are also made into wine, such as Alphonse Lavallée in Bali (the only variety available locally) and Chasselas in Switzerland (because it grows quickly, despite the cold climate).

Rootstock varieties, with technical references (e.g. 34EM for "École de Montpellier"), are chosen for their resistance to phylloxera and adaptation to different soils. Although all these "American" varieties are resistant to the insect, some grow better in limestone, others in sandy soil … so a choice has to be made when planting a vineyard.

Although it is sometimes difficult to recognise a variety just by looking at the vine, the spring growth of some plantations differentiates them visually. The leaves of the early varieties appear first, whereas the late varieties take time to mature and are well suited to hot climates.

International varieties are French local varieties that became famous in Bordeaux (Merlot, Cabernet Franc, Sauvignon), Burgundy and Champagne (Chardonnay, Pinot Noir) and so were tried out by winemakers around the world. It's easy to get your message across using these names known to everybody. The disadvantage is a certain standardisation of taste, which some call "Coca-Cola wine", even though this standardisation is caused more by winemaking techniques.

Local, *indigenous* or *native* varieties grew in each region before the winemakers uprooted them in favour of better-known and more highly valued international varieties. These days, encouraging them may seem like a separatist or nationalist statement.

The so-called *forgotten* varieties were once well known. But disease, changing consumer tastes, legislation and profitability led to their disappearance, sometimes forever. By definition they're difficult to track down and list. They catch the palate unawares. Exclamations of surprise like "Wow! I see why they've been forgotten" are sometimes heard at tastings. Maybe the vinification was inappropriate or unsuccessful.

If we counted all the various hybrids of wild, American and European vines, there would be over 10,000 varieties worldwide, many of which are similar although known by different names.

NB: *variety* (of grape) is not a synonym for *varietal*, a term that relates to a wine made predominantly from a single grape variety.

In France, the ten most common grape varieties occupy 71 per cent of the plantations. In order of importance, they are: Merlot, Grenache, Ugni Blanc (for cognac), Syrah, Cabernet Sauvignon, Chardonnay, Carignan, Cabernet Franc, Pinot Noir and Sauvignon (*source*: www.observatoire-viti-france.com). Note that the official *Catalogue des variétés et clones de vines cultivées en France* only authorises 341 varieties, plus various American rootstocks adapted to different soils.

Each country and each region has its specificities. In Sicily, the ten most popular varieties cover 78 per cent of the cultivated area, but are all quite different. In order of importance: Catarratto Bianco Comune, Nero d'Avola, Catarratto Bianco Lucido, Inzolia, Grillo, Trebbiano Toscano, Syrah, Chardonnay, Merlot and Grecanico.

A monovarietal Bordeaux

**Rare example of Bordeaux wine
made from a single grape variety in a world
where blending different varieties is the norm**

Just as an orchestra brings together several instruments, a perfumer blends different fragrances and a painter chooses a range of colours from his palette, the Bordeaux cellar masters are conductors, perfumers and artists. To make a red Bordeaux, they blend grape varieties that are authorised in the appellation zone: Merlot, Cabernet Sauvignon, Cabernet Franc and Malbec, plus a few rarities known as Petit Verdot, Villard Noir, Carménère and Fer Servadou. The first three account for 99 per cent of red grape plantations.

Each variety is harvested at maturity and the grapes are fermented in separate vats. After careful consideration and testing, the final selection of varieties is blended during an operation called *assemblage*, each vat lending its qualities to the desired balance of the finished wine. Watch your language here: the words *mélange* (mixture) and *coupage* (cut) are pejorative and imply mediocre wines, whereas *assemblage* is nobler.

Even in the appellations where a single variety is used – Pinot Noir in Burgundy, Gamay in Beaujolais – the plots within a holding are fermented separately, according to their maturity (which is linked to the climate and *terroir*), and are usually blended by the winegrowers. The quality of the ingredients is reflected in the finished product.

Tasting different vats and blending trials, Rocaudy estate, Languedoc (France)

In the Bordeaux region of France, this tradition of blending different varieties dates back to the time when white and red grapes were pressed together to obtain *clairet* (claret) that was exported by ship to England and other northern countries. Growers know that it's best "not to put all your eggs in one basket" and to cultivate varieties with different flowering times and susceptibilities, thus reducing the risks associated with heavy rainfall or disease.

After the phylloxera disaster at the end of the 19th century, the Carménère grape seemed to be extinct. In 1991, however, a root was found in Chile. Although this low-yielding variety is sensitive to *coulure* (poor fruit set when rain washes away the pollen), a few Bordeaux winegrowers replanted it anyway.

Today, with his *Pure Carménère*, Henri Duporge turns his back on the idea of blending. The wine is a monovarietal (from a single grape variety) with low yields (20 hectolitres per hectare), produced organically and free from chemicals.

A vine classified as a historic monument

A vineyard planted in Gers (France) around 1820

Uniquely, crops have now been listed on the French Inventory of Historic Monuments: this family garden at Sarragachies in Val d'Adour (Gers) was spared by phylloxera … and from being uprooted.

"My grandmother's grandmother said they were already old vines," recounts René Pédebernade who, at 87 years of age, was still attaching the vines to stakes with wicker as his ancestors had always done. Each Sarragachies family used to have its own "vine garden" planted with different red and white local varieties and produced its own wine – "garage wine", as we'd say today.

This recently listed garden has several striking features. A quick glance reveals an ancient plantation in double rows, with the same stake supporting two plants, perhaps to save materials. The vines are arranged in 2 metre squares so that draft horses or oxen could pass by on all sides.

Experts from Sup Agro Montpellier, the Institut Français de la Vigne et du Vin (IFV) and the Institut National de la Recherche Agronomique (INRA) believe that the plantation dates from around 1820, and its sandy soil prevented the spread of phylloxera.

Finally, genetic analysis of these living relics reveals twenty different grape varieties, including seven that were completely unknown.

These vestiges survived uprooting because the family garden was not obliged to make a profit or follow new trends. Elsewhere the vines were replaced, either because the yield or the alcohol level was too low, or the growers complied with the authorised and certified clones. In the 1980s, the move to *appellation d'origine* was the motivation for uprooting and replanting many plots of land. Market forces, government incentives and agricultural advisers destroyed as much as phylloxera did. Like a thousand other viticulturists, Jean-Pascal Pédebernade – René's son – sells his grapes to Plaimont Producteurs. "We wanted to save these ancient vines for two reasons," reveals Olivier Bourdet-Pees, the cooperative's general manager. "We defend the local varieties because they have developed in local conditions, with the peculiarities of the terrain and climate. These varieties are adapted to our rainfall, which averages 1,000 millimetres a year. In 1950, the twenty most popular grape varieties accounted for 47 per cent of production, but today it's 86 per cent!" The genetic heritage and biodiversity are collapsing.

One of these unknown grape varieties found on Sarragachies land, known as Pédebernade No. 1, was tested in a micro-winemaking experiment. It yielded a wine of only 7° alcohol. For Bourdet-Pees, this is a hopeful sign: "In Norway, the tax goes up with the level of alcohol. Low-alcohol wine is a future option." So some people have understood that biodiversity favours adaptation to a changing and diverse market, new consumption patterns and global warming.

Male and female vines, in a wine-producing world where all currently registered varieties are hermaphrodite

At Sarragachies, there are even male vines – without grapes – and female vines. For a long time, growers have selected plants with the reproductive parts of both sexes: male (to fertilise) and female (to produce the clusters of grapes). So all currently registered varieties are hermaphrodite: neither male nor female.

Vino della pace: a "peace wine" blended from 600 varieties from the five continents

"All the flavours of the Earth in a glass"

The Friuli region of Italy, lying between Slovenia, the Alps and the Adriatic, is where Latin, Slavic and Germanic cultures intermingle, as shown on a map of grape varieties: the plantations of Merlot, Cabernet Franc, Pinot Blanc and Pinot Gris evoke the Napoleonic era and the years of French occupation, while the decorated barrels at the Cormons cooperative show that eastern Friuli was part of Austria until 1919.

The local varieties are so numerous (Verduzzo, Refosco, Picolit …) that a grower has difficulty in choosing which to plant. This abundance complicates the work of wine experts, who need to know the varieties of the appellation zone and their specific problems, in particular phytosanitary requirements, in the absence of scientific studies. Biodiversity can also affect the marketing of a wine: how to explain to a potential buyer the differences in the characteristics of each vintage?

To overcome the problems posed by this diversity, the Friulians turned all this to their advantage and got their message across. Unlike the Italian tradition of naming a wine after its place of origin or *terroir*, Friuli labels indicate the grape variety. One of the specialities of the region's nurseries, at Rauscedo, has become the propagation of multiple varieties.

But the most spectacular initiative comes from the Cormons cooperative. Every year since 1983, its 200 members and international guests gather to harvest the 3-hectare heritage plot where 600 varieties from around the world have been planted: Syrah, Tulilah, Shurrebe, Pedral, Maizy, Marzemino, Terrano, Merlot, Gamay, Ucelut ... Pressed and fermented together, they produce a white "peace wine", which brings together "all the flavours of the Earth in a glass".

These bottles with their artist's labels, packed in handsome wooden crates, are sent to embassies and heads of state around the world "as a gift to promote friendship and good relations with Italy".

Sinefinis: a political wine

A wine from the Italy/Slovenia border is a reminder that this was one land before Yugoslavia was created

The wine known as *Sinefinis* means "without end, without borders": aiming to symbolically reunite that same *terroir* separated just after the Second World War (Italy on one side and Yugoslavia on the other), it blends the production of a Slovenian and an Italian winemaker.

The land was even part of Austria until 1919, and then it was Italian until 1947 when the Iron Curtain came down.

Producing the same local grape – known as Rumena Rebula or Ribolla Gialla depending on which side of the border it's grown – the Slovenian Matjaz Četrtič of the Ferdinand estate and the Italian Robert Princic da Giasbana of Gradis'ciutta have pooled their agricultural and commercial expertise, taken a Master's in the wine business and planned their *Sinefinis* wine. "This transborder sparkling wine will of course be classified as a *vin de table*, but we'll explain our method on the label. The acidity of the Rebula is well suited to it."

Although the basic wine is made at each vineyard, refining is a joint venture. This somewhat unlikely relationship aims to demonstrate that it is the same wine-producing region divided in two: the appellation is *Brda* in Slovenia and *Collio* in Italy. Wine can carry a political message too.

Geopolitics also dictated the choice of grape variety, explains Toni Gomiscek, director of Vinoteka Brda, the largest selection of wines in the zone. He sees this as an example of the absurd legacy of totalitarian regimes: "In the Austro-Hungarian era, red wine was the priority because we were located in the south of the empire. That's normal: red is planted in the south. Then when we became Italians, we were obliged to plant white varieties. Logical: we'd become the north of the country!" The white Rebula grape is still grown there.

View of the valley from the Ferdinand estate

Rare or forgotten varieties

As market forces change, some varieties disappear and others come back into fashion

The vine has three unique characteristics: its varieties have noticeable differences, the plants are easily crossed, and the life of rootstock can exceed tens or even hundreds of years. So within the same species of *Vitis vinifera* there is immense biodiversity, and not only in skin colour.

In the mid-19th century, powdery mildew (oidium) spores forced growers to replant their vineyards with varieties that were less sensitive to this pathology. Soon afterwards, with phylloxera (the insect that gave its name to the disease), they developed resistant hybrid vines from local varieties crossed with American varieties, or local varieties grafted onto American rootstock. Thousands of local curiosities disappeared in this way, wiped out by epidemics or the hand of man, and the extraordinary biodiversity declined.

Some varieties were also consigned to oblivion because they failed to produce a good crop, or on the other hand produced too much. The alcohol content of others was too low: these varieties are now used to make wines with a low alcohol content, which attracts lower taxes in some countries, for example in Scandinavia. Today, it is not for nostalgic reasons or as collectors' items that rare varieties are sought out, but because their biodiversity results in unusual flavours and aromas, provides solutions to technical problems or disease, or responds to changes in demand.

Oidium (powdery mildew) on the vine

Among countless abandoned local varieties, the Abrostine (or Abrusca) of Tuscany was well known at the time of the Etruscans. Used as medication or to fortify Tuscan wines, it was overlooked because of a low yield, but has now been rescued by the universities of Pisa and Florence, which have preserved several ancient varieties as part of a European programme.

Another completely different reason for dropping a variety is overproduction. The Aramon grape, which is relatively resistant to powdery mildew, gives a vast quantity of watery wine that is supple and easy to drink (up to 300 quintals per hectare if the vines are irrigated and fertilised, i.e. 3 kilos of grapes per square metre). During peaks of overproduction, this variety was banned from "quality wine" designations but it can be cultivated at lower yields of higher quality, using for example organic methods with no chemical fertilisers.

Well-known appellations also have their forgotten varieties. Although Pinot Noir, Pinot Meunier (also dark-skinned) and Chardonnay (white) cover more than 99.7 per cent of the Champagne vineyards, other varieties are authorised, such as Arbane, Petit Meslier, Pinot Blanc and Pinot Gris, although they represent only 0.3 per cent of the total. For its *Quattuor* (with two *t*s) vintage, the Drappier estate blends equal parts of Chardonnay, true Pinot Blanc, Petit Meslier and the very rare Arbane. The wines are kept in cellars founded by the local abbey at Clairvaux.

At his winery in the Rhone valley, the Belgian former motor-racing champion Dirk Vermeersch cultivates Aramon and Alicante Bouchet grapes from vines planted in 1946 and which are not entitled to the Côtes du Rhône appellation. So he's making a simple "*vin de France*" whose interest lies in these rare varieties.

Federico Staderini, a veritable roving oenologist, uses local varieties in his *Sempremai*, Toscana IGT vintage (Tuscany, Italy).

Known as the "wine-producers' Louvre", the INRA conservatory at Marseillan in the Languedoc region of France, maintains 7,500 different varieties in sandy soil that was spared by phylloxera. The conservatory is due to be moved to a different site – to the consternation of vine lovers.

In the private sector, one of the largest stocks belongs to Plaimont Producteurs.

Accursed, banned and mythical varieties

Banned then reinstated, "the wine that blinds you, the wine that makes you deaf, the wine that drives you mad" have almost completely disappeared

Among the great diversity of grape varieties grown in France, six were sentenced to death by the law of 24 December 1934: "It is forbidden to sell on the domestic market, as well as purchase, transport or plant the varieties listed below, whatever the local names given to them: Noah, Othello, Isabella, Jacquez, Clinton, Herbemont." They're all hybrids, i.e. crosses of American and European grape varieties, grown at the time for their resistance to phylloxera.

Two reasons were cited during the debate to justify this ban: the alleged revolting taste and the health hazard posed by these varieties. The "revolting taste" refers to the particular flavour, known as "foxy" in both grapes and wine, somewhere between raspberry and the supposed musty odour of fox.

As for the "health hazard", fermentation of the Noah grape does in fact generate ether and some methyl alcohol (methanol). In high doses, this is lethal to the optic nerve, hence the legend of a wine that makes you blind. One hybrid, Baco, is still authorised and yields a wine that isn't for consumption but for distillation in the production of Armagnac.

In reality, this prohibition was a political decision brought on by an economic crisis. Around 1934, French winemakers were overproducing. The shortage due to phylloxera was past and hybrids of American vines, which were resistant to the disease, were extremely high yielding.

The other method of overcoming phylloxera (grafting onto American rootstock) was also used and the plains of Languedoc, planted with grafted Aramon vines, were also very productive: over 30,000 litres of red wine per hectare, or 3 litres to the square metre, thanks to irrigation. A colossal yield.

Another reason for the surplus was the French colonists in Algeria, who invested in vineyards as far as the eye could see. Planted and tended by an underpaid workforce, they also benefited from tax breaks. According to Freddy Couderc (author of *Les vins mythiques de la Cévenne ardéchoise et du Bas-Vivarais*, published by La Mirandole), Algerian production rose from 221,000 hectolitres in 1928 to 373,000 hectolitres in 1934: "In the *département* of Oran alone, from 1931 to 1933, the surface area of vineyards increased by 11,000 hectares." These new vineyards swamped the French market with millions of litres of cheap wine.

This surplus caused prices to collapse and threatened to ruin hundreds of thousands of winegrowers and their families. The French National Assembly feared a revolt, so it sacrificed six very productive hybrid varieties, all derived from crosses with New World vines. Henceforth the only authorised vines were European varieties (Merlot, Syrah, Chardonnay ...), grafted onto American rootstock that was resistant to phylloxera.

Couderc explains how these banned hybrid varieties attained mythical status in the Cévennes: "The flagship wine of resistance, of lost causes, of anarchists, the prohibited wine par excellence. With its sentimental associations with the mining region, it became the symbol of the suffering and struggling Cévennes as it captured people's imagination."

Although this ban on hybrids was lifted in 2003, the varieties in question had almost all disappeared in less than seventy years. But a few survived among vines grown for domestic use. They can be found in unconventional networks that encourage the rediscovery of forgotten fruits.

Hybrid varieties were also banned in 1930s' Italy. The Isabella grape (Uva Fragola or "strawberry grape") avoided this ban and some winemakers are still using it.

Wines from interplanted vines

Planting different varieties in the same vineyard has many advantages

Interplanting brings together different plant species or varieties in the same plot. The practice goes back to antiquity, when planters were already taking advantage of the space between vines and olive trees to grow cereals and vegetables.

This probably began when different grape varieties were planted to select those suitable for the climate and *terroir*. The most adaptable thrived to form a collection of plants of great diversity which was guaranteed to yield mature grapes and wine every year.

Biodiversity is an insurance policy for the winegrower: poor weather during flowering won't condemn the whole vineyard, if it's interplanted, because the time of flowering depends on the variety. Similarly, a disease doesn't affect all plants in the same way, so will spread more slowly. The only problem is that as the grapes don't all ripen at the same time, the winemaker's skill lies in either choosing the harvest date so that there's a balance between sweet and acid grapes, or harvesting in several passes, each time picking the ripest grapes.

Gemischter Satz ("mixed set") vines in Vienna

With interplanting, the winemaker also dictates the ingredients and proportions of the finished blends. The recipe is written in the soil with pick and shovel, to be handed on like an heirloom. Interplanting guarantees the transmission of a particular style of wine. A modern version is Bourgogne Passe-Tout-Grains, where the vineyard brings together one-third Pinot Noir and two-thirds Gamay (at least one plant or one row in three of Pinot Noir – a maximum of two plants or two rows in three of Gamay). The whole lot is harvested, pressed and fermented together. The appellation also authorises additional white varieties, limited to 15 per cent: Chardonnay, Pinot Blanc and Pinot Gris. So the blend is created in the vineyard.

Although nowadays a wine that blends several varieties is rarely derived from interplanting, a few growers continue this tradition and plant different grapes in the same row, or one row in two, or three, or four. In some countries, such as Croatia, gardeners also alternate vines with other vegetables.

In Alsace, the tradition of interplanting was banned after the 1871 annexation, when the Germans imposed a monovarietal system to control the winemakers' activities. At Bergheim, in the heart of the Alsace vineyards, Jean-Michel Deiss has nevertheless reinstated the tradition, starting with thirteen local varieties harvested, pressed and fermented together. "These grapes express Alsatian plurality and we're happy to produce a wine that speaks of our commitment to our region, its grape varieties and traditions."

The traditional white wine of Vienna (Austria), *Gemischter Satz*, is a blend of three to twenty varieties grown on the same plot, and harvested and fermented together. Each plays a specific role: Pinot Blanc and Riesling provide the base, the Rhine Riesling gives acidity, Muscat and Traminer their aromatic strength, each plot producing an original and unique wine.

Roses planted at the end of rows of vines are another example of interplanting. They play a triple role: attractive to look at, they were formerly used to warn the grower of powdery mildew (the rose is susceptible to the disease); and the thorns discouraged horses from turning too sharply and damaging the last vine in the row.

Châteauneuf-du-Pape *Paule Courtil* combines the thirteen grape varieties authorised in its appellation zone, some of which have virtually disappeared: Grenache, Mourvèdre, Syrah, Cinsault, Roussanne, Muscardin, Counoise, Clairette, Bourboulenc, Piquepoul, Picardan, Vaccarèse and Terret Noir. This Côtes-du-Rhône is produced by Gerard Jacumin, winemaker at Châteauneuf-du-Pape. The wine is named after his wife, Paule Courtil.

In the Minervois (Languedoc-Roussillon region of France), Patricia Boyer-Domergue also domesticates forgotten rootstocks: "Time to browse through ancient vines, mark the unknown varieties, have them identified, recuperate the wood, check their state of health and then propagate them … *C de Centeilles* is the high point of a winegrower's life." This red vintage is a blend of rare, maybe unique, varieties: Piquepoul Noir (78 per cent), Riveirenc Noir (15 per cent), Morastel Noir with its white juice (5 per cent) and Oeillade (2 per cent). To preserve these forgotten flavours, the wines are not stored in barrels.

PIWI grapes

To avoid the use of pesticides, some growers are helping to develop fungus-resistant varieties

Treatments against the fungal spores of mildew and oidium, which attack at times of high humidity, mainly involve spraying synthetic pesticides that are toxic to the ecosystem and to the growers themselves. Although organic viticulture is limited to more traditional substances (sulphur, copper sulphate ...), these elements accumulate in the soil: you only need to look at the turquoise colour, due to copper, of any wall behind a vine.

Finally, repeated passes of the tractor for spraying – whether organic or conventional – burn fuel and compact the soil.

For a solution, we must go back to basics.

In the wild, the vine propagates itself in two different ways: sexual reproduction (pollination of female flowers by male flowers) or layering, when the flexible stem of the creeper drops to the ground and generates new roots. Fertilisation of the flowers produces grapes and fertile seeds, which become individuals that differ slightly from their parentage. Layering, on the other hand, leads to a clone, an identical copy. This was once the chosen method for perpetuating listed varieties, which are nowadays propagated by grafting. A small stem is cut from one plant and inserted within the rootstock tissue of another, where it develops into a new plant. Layering is still sometimes practised in phylloxera-free regions.

The way to obtain new disease-resistant vines, with no need for pesticides, is to renew their genetic makeup (avoiding GM). Rather than identical clones produced by layering, taking cuttings or conventional grafting, new lines are selected by sexual reproduction, through pollination of the vine. In countries where the wine-producing regulations allow, researchers create and select hybrids known as *pilzwiderstandsfähig* (resistant to fungal diseases – abbreviated to PIWI). In the 19th century, hybridisation was the foremost answer to phylloxera.

In countries such as France, each appellation zone draws up a list of authorised varieties, excluding these hybrids. In France, a wine from PIWI vines will thus have to be classified as ordinary *vin de table*.

PIWI International brings together researchers, growers, viticultural nurseries, selectors and members of institutions from a dozen countries. It organises a competition so that professionals and the public can discover the diversity and interest of wines from these resistant plants.

One of the few estates still creating new varieties in France – La Colombette in the Languedoc – is run by father and son François and Vincent Pugibet: "Today, vines are propagated by grafting, asexually. This gives homogeneous lines, but doesn't let the plant evolve along with its environment."

"Our project is to return to sexual reproduction, by flowers. Given a wise choice of parent plants, the seeds obtained from their descendants combine resistance and organoleptic qualities. These far from standard varieties have some famous ancestors such as Chardonnay or Cabernet; others have a more inflammatory past such as Maréchal Foch; some have unknown or unpronounceable names such as Kishmish Vatkana; some are anonymous progenitors, simply passing on their resistance, or wild plants from distant lands such as Amurensis or Caribaea; or again some are unsuspected adulterers, finally welcome. This extensive interbreeding has produced original grape varieties, all grouped under the PIWI label."

These "experimental vines" are responsible for La Colombette's *Au creux du nid* vintages, classified as *"vin de France"* with no appellation zone. The white comes from the "mainly cal06-04" variety and the red from a mysterious "Cabernet Jura". And it works: "The vines at La Colombette aren't treated – no copper, no sulphites – and the wines produced are highly rated award-winners," confirm Pugibet father and son.

With 20 varieties planted over 30 hectares, the Pugibets have encouraged other estates to follow suit, such as Ducourt vineyards (3 hectares) and the Cuisset family (1.5 hectares) in the Entre-Deux-Mers and Bergerac regions of France respectively.

Variety cal06-04

Work in the vineyard: unconventional plantations and staggered harvests

"I know thou labourest on the hill of fire,
In sweat and pain beneath a flaming sun,
To give the life and soul my vines desire ..."
Charles Baudelaire, L'âme du vin (The Soul of Wine, trans. F. P. Sturm)

"Whenever I see a vine, I think of wine," claims Mario Falcetti, manager of Quadra Franciacorta.

Great winegrowers know how to organise a vineyard depending on the grapes and the type of wine they want to produce. The initial choice of varieties, winter pruning, cropping (cutting the tops off the stems), training the vines, the green harvest, all the work of the vineyard influences the amount and quality of the resulting wine. A good grower plays on this range of variables. So cropping some of the excess foliage lets the vine sap reach the grapes. Stems neatly arranged along wires, with not too many leaves, help the grapes to dry faster after rain or morning mist, so there's less risk of mildew. Tying up the stems is in itself a phytosanitary measure.

Green harvesting is done to eliminate some of the grapes so that the sap feeds only the best. As the quantity decreases the quality and ripeness increase, together with the sugar level and potential alcohol. A pair of secateurs is the first determining factor in the alcohol content of a wine.

Winegrowers – some of them anyway – are among the few farmers proud of their low yields. Although *appellations d'origine* (AOC or DOC) limit production per hectare, some growers further reduce the volume they harvest.

Harvesting "en hautain" (at great height, the vines attached to trees), 18th century

Uprooting vines to prepare the ground for a new plantation, Rocaudy (Languedoc, France)

Of course, everything depends on the region and the desired wine. In Bali, the tropical climate guarantees high yields. In Champagne, the climate isn't exactly conducive to ripening grapes but high yields with a degree of acidity are sought to give a refreshing wine. This is a far cry from the wines of Frank Cornelissen in Sicily, who even refuses to work the soil between the vines "because it stimulates bacterial life and increases the yield. At only 10 quintals (1 tonne) of grapes per hectare, my vineyard is healthy and disease free. The vine has to look after itself – the same goes for my wine, which is preserved without sulphites." So no fertilisers or treatments are used, giving a very low yield of around 1,000 to 2,000 bottles per hectare, five times less than might be expected.

Vines live at their own pace, depending on the growing cycle. Unlike dairy herds that have to be milked twice a day, a vine can be left for a week, or a couple of months in winter, without a visit. It knows how to feed itself and soon takes over, launching its serpentine branches in the direction of the surrounding vegetation, clinging wherever it can. It doesn't need the hand of man.

A walk through a vineyard helps understanding of what type of wine will be produced. Is the space between the rows ploughed up, or covered with short grass? If the land is arid, perhaps the grower wants the vines to benefit from all the rainwater, without other plants taking their share. Conversely, some growers let the grass grow to compete with the vine and so reduce the yield. Others plough every other row – one row of grass to maintain biodiversity and insect life, one row of bare earth so that water penetrates and nourishes the vines.

The winegrower's year is not limited to one spectacular and brief harvest. Throughout the year, the developing rootstocks have to be attended to. In winter, when the leaves have fallen and the stems are almost dried out to better withstand the frost, pruning the plant down to just two or three stems drastically reduces its size. By pruning short or long, the grower is already determining the yield of the next harvest. No plant is identical and each of course demands the personal touch.

Legend has it that pruning was invented by a donkey that took the liberty of nibbling at his master's vine. Although the owner was furious at the sight of his mutilated plant, he realised six months later that it yielded fewer grapes, but they were beautifully sweet.

Depending on the methods adopted in the vineyard, labels on the bottles may carry the words "raisonnée" (from lutte raisonnée, literally "reasoned struggle", or "supervised control", indicating sustainability), "organic" or "biodynamic". Raisonnée is meaningless, however, because every farmer has, since the dawn of time, calculated the benefits and risks of any decision. Similarly, the expression "respects the environment" guarantees nothing much. Only "organic" or "bio" guarantees compliance with the requirements of an organic certifying agency that the wine is free from chemical fertilisers or synthetic pesticides, and that natural methods and lower yields to strengthen the vines have been used. This type of wine is said to be "from organic grapes". Since the 2012 harvest, the new European regulations for organic wine take into account the production methods at the winery.

This aspect is all the more important because, like all fruit producers, conventional winegrowers use vast quantities of pesticides. The biodynamic method seems more arcane: spraying plants with herbal diffusions on certain days and at certain times, following the phases of the moon. The methods also vary: some growers object to cutting back the stems to stop growth (you wouldn't cut the whiskers from a cat or the horns from cattle or snails, after all), so they tie them up instead.

When nothing is specified on the label, the wine may be from a conventional vineyard, but it could also be organic because growers may use organic methods without mentioning it. Some organic wines with a strange taste have in fact put people off, to the extent that the "organic" label may actually be counter-productive. Fortunately a number of wine competitions, such as Amphore in France, give awards to delicious organic wines.

Organic, no herbicides
Angélica Oury (Rocaudy) weeding by hand

Vineyard music

"The vine whisperer"

A number of growers have installed loudspeakers in their vineyards. Among the best known is Giancarlo Cignozzi, of the Paradiso di Frassina estate in Tuscany (Italy). This former lawyer has managed to convince Bose Corporation to provide enough speakers so that his estate is awash with sound. He broadcasts various genres of music over the seasons: sacred in winter, Baroque and Vivaldi in spring ... Two researchers, Stefano Mancuso from the University of Florence, and Andrea Lucchi from the University of Pisa, are studying the effect on vine growth and insect infestations. The results are encouraging, both for promoting growth and for resistance to disease.

On the publicity front, Cignozzi has earned himself an international reputation. "The vine whisperer" poetically compares the grape varieties to the different characters in Mozart operas: brought together in a blend, these grapes/characters all have their role to play.

The music plays on an endless loop in the vineyards that produce the *Flauto Magico* (Magic Flute) vintage. "An austere wine but with soft and elegant tannins ... Thanks to Amadeus? I think so – but you be the judge!" One of his labels depicts the grapes as so many notes on a stave. Another of his wines, *12 UVE*, associates twelve varieties with the twelve notes of the chromatic scale.

Other French wineries are also experimenting with music. The Génodics company cites over 200 installations in vineyards, market gardens and farms where sound waves are used for therapeutic purposes. Physicist Joël Sternheimer has observed that the biosynthesis of the proteins that make up every living being is associated with frequencies and rhythms, which he calls *protéodies* ("protein melodies"). A sound sequence could act on this synthesis, stimulate or inhibit an amino acid, regulate biological processes, strengthen natural resistance, and treat viral, bacterial or fungal diseases. According to Michel Loriot, president of Vignerons Indépendants de Champagne: "Music for plants broadcast through my vines gives the grapes better resistance to disease and allows them to thrive." Esca, the devastating fungus that attacks the woody stems of the vines, also seems to be held at bay with this treatment.

www.alparadisodifrassina.it

Music in the cellars

Michel Loriot also practises music therapy in his cellars: "The greatest composers nurture the bottled wines: they ferment for two months to the strains of Beethoven's Pastoral Symphony. Then Mozart, Brahms, Mahler, Vivaldi and Elgar turn up to join in the magic of effervescence. The vibrations of the notes reach the wine, its yeasts and proteins. They affect its structure and help to bring out all its flavours and aromas during the ageing process."

Biodynamic winemaker Nicolas Joly uses a minimalist technique: "It's better to strike a single note with a tuning fork in the tank."

Some winemakers also play the violin or accordion to their casks or sound a hunting horn on the slopes.

www.champagne-michelloriot.com

The effect of music at tastings

Music also alters our intellectual perception and influences our sense of taste. Ophelia Deroy, researcher at the Centre for the Study of the Senses at the University of London, describes such an experiment: "Participants who were tasting wines to the voices of *Carmina Burana* judged these wines to be more characterful than did those people who were tasting them to the accompaniment of other music. Conversely, the wines were judged more dynamic and refreshing when served in a room where Depeche Mode's *Just Can't Get Enough* – itself fresh and dynamic – was playing."

But don't overdo it: stimulating too many senses at once (taste, vision, hearing ...) may ruin your concentration and the perception that a tasting session demands. Serving wine against a background of images and sounds may overwhelm the target audience with too much information, or even prejudge the outcome.

Plenty of festivals associate music with wine. Some music-loving winetasters recommend a particular track to accompany a certain bottle. This is often personal taste, but the analogy between the sensations of hearing and drinking can sometimes be expressed in eloquent terms. A notable example being the *sonorités aromatiques* ("aromatic tones") of Frédéric Beneix and Marien Nègre of Wine4Melomanes, Château La Croix du Merle (Saint-Émilion). The estate also plays music in its vineyards and winery.
www.wine4melomanes.com

Disturbing links between music and vines

In their vocabulary, tasters distinguish notes (woody, spicy …), evoking the opening, finish and harmony, the range of the wines. They estimate a wine's finish by the number of seconds (caudalie)* a sensation persists in the mouth – the silence after Mozart is still Mozart. The shape of a glass and the acoustics of a concert hall are comparable, as these two spaces can enhance or disturb the work of the winemaker as conductor.

For thousands of years grapes have been trodden by foot, with or without boots, to the rhythm of work songs accompanying the winery tasks. In France, this habit of singing at work died out after the 1914–18 war. The wine reserved for Mass was accompanied by hymns, while banquets resounded to drinking songs.

"The score is written on the ground," says Jacques Puisais, oenologist and philosopher, founder of the French *Institut* du *Goût* (association dedicated to an appreciation of taste). As a visual analogy: along the rows of vines, the training wires look like a musical score on which the clusters of grapes hang like notes. Sparkling wine is the most voluble. Uncorking a bottle is the opportunity for an explosive sound, which sophisticated hosts avoid because they prefer the discreet murmur of bubbles. The sound of a cork popping is still the finest argument in favour of traditional corks rather than aluminium caps.

*Derived from caudal (tail), this is the unit used to measure the persistence of a wine's finish (1 caudalie represents 1 second).

The *alberello* vines of Pantelleria

The first traditional vinegrowing practice to be listed by UNESCO

In late November 2014, the representatives of 161 states voted unanimously to register the cultivation of bush vines trained low on the ground with no trellising (*vite ad alberello*) on the Mediterranean island of Pantelleria as Intangible Cultural Heritage. This UNESCO list of local traditions, festivals and performances is now open to outstanding agricultural practices.

The 8,300-hectare Italian island of Pantelleria, which is closer to Tunisia (72 kilometres) than it is to Sicily (100 kilometres), has been transformed into a garden paradise over centuries of hard work by the inhabitants. On this virtually uncultivable land, studded with volcanic rocks, successive generations have built thousands of kilometres of retaining walls with little terraces where a few vines or caper shrubs grow. The island resembles an ancient city where only the walls are left standing.

The challenge was enormous: no rain (barely 300 millimetres, almost exclusively in winter), and a burning, sand-laden wind (the sirocco) that dries up the foliage, disrupts flowering and fertilisation and damages the fruit when it does grow.

Under this African sun there are no sources of fresh water, just sulphurous volcanic springs that are full of minerals, thermal, undrinkable. Impossible to irrigate. In case of fire there's only seawater, which would damage the crops.

For centuries the island was also prey to pirates because of its strategic position.

The islanders survived by building Mediterranean-style houses known as *dammusi*. Their domed roof terraces catch the winter rainfall and the water is stored in underground cisterns. Traditionally, the narrow windows gave protection from the wind and any marauders; at night, the shutters hid the glow of the lights inside.

Drying grapes, De Bartoli estate

Passerillage (drying grapes on the vine) at Carole Bouquet's

Preparing Passito, Donnafugata estate

Walls that are constantly repaired and extended supported the small gardens. Towers several metres high, known as "Arab gardens", were built to protect each orange tree, each lemon tree, from the wind. Pantelleria really does raise its fruit trees with the same care as livestock for an agricultural show: the sloping tops of the walls direct the least drop of rain inside the garden.

At Pantelleria, the plants have lost the habit of taking in water through their roots. They absorb it through their leaves, from the condensation caused by the temperature difference between night and day in the humid marine climate. This phenomenon occurs inside the high walls of the Arab gardens, as well as in every hollow dug out to plant a vine, pruned *ad alberello* (goblet), whose stems creep along the ground. This humble *alberello* technique, the symbol of a cultivation system that is as laborious as it is ingenious, is now part of the Intangible Cultural Heritage of humanity.

For centuries the farmers cultivated grapes in order to export raisins. Now they produce *Passito di Pantelleria*, a naturally sweet white wine paradoxically flowing from such a harsh island, and a dry white. Passito is obtained by adding raisins to the fermenting juice, as in Hungary's *Tokaji Aszú*.

Pantelleria, a rural community on the fringes of Africa, is now a resort for jet-set socialites: Carole Bouquet has bought an estate and produces the *Sangue d'oro* label; Gérard Depardieu has lived there; Giorgio Armani, Sting and Madonna like to visit. The new UNESCO status will enhance the reputation of the island's wines.

New Year's Eve harvests

Every 31 December, the growers of Plaimont Producteurs end the year with a festival and nocturnal harvests open to all

Viella (Gers, France). Over 500 visitors, young and old, are warming themselves over burning branches. At 7.30 in the evening they grab their secateurs and baskets for the final harvest of the year: a half-hour by candlelight before rejoining their respective celebrations. Members of the Plaimont Producteurs cooperative are proud to show off their craft and launch the New Year festivities.

The *Pacherenc de la Saint-Sylvestre* vintage was launched in 1991 when the viticulturists, caught out by an exceptional frost, decided to leave the grapes on the vine until 31 December.

Dried by the wind, exposed to the autumn sun and cold nights, the sugars concentrate in the grapes, preventing them from freezing. The skin thickens as they mature, so they keep longer on the vine. In other appellation zones, this *passerillage** is carried out in a barn or shed with the clusters hung on wires.

The vines of the *Pacherenc du Vic-Bihl* zone cover 250 hectares between Gers, the Pyrénées-Atlantiques and the Hautes-Pyrénées. The grape varieties are local – Petit and Gros Manseng. From October to December, in four or five passes (*tries*), the growers harvest the ripe grapes for different wines and the grape juice is fermented to medium-sweet (*moelleux*) depending on the batch. The October grape yields aromas of fresh fruits, citrus, grapefruit; the November grape (around St Albert's Day) evokes candied fruits, spices; the December grape is reminiscent of dried fruits – almonds, walnuts, honey … Thanks to the acidity of these varieties and the cool climate, the wine remains balanced and not too sweet. A medium-sweet redolent with flavour and history.

*French term relating to grapes that have been dried ("raisined") on the vine, to concentrate the sugars.

This harvest festival was originally held even later, after midnight on 31 December. The Plaimont cooperative used to erect a marquee to accommodate the revellers, but this was expensive in both rent and insurance and a heavy workload for the volunteers. Nowadays the harvest begins in the early evening, so children can take part. It's no longer the first harvest of the year, but the last. The celebrations begin in the morning with a snack among the vines that will be harvested that evening. Demonstrations by draught horses evoke the work of bygone days, while winemakers tell of their craft and show visitors around the rows of vines, covered with netting to protect them from hungry birds. You can taste the overripe grapes to enjoy their sugar content. The village resonates to the sound of wandering musicians and local versions of *boules* such as *jeu de quilles* and *palet gascon*, while horse-drawn carriages offer rides. Vine grafters, wood turners, wool spinners, grinders and *espélouquères* (who strip the cobs from the corn) all demonstrate their age-old skills to the new generations. Not to mention tasting the different *tries* of *Pacherenc* and other wines.

Vineyard horses

In recent years a few growers have again turned to traditional equine labour

Excavations of the vineyards at Pompeii have revealed that draught animals were widely used to work the vines, as borne out in Pliny the Elder's *Natural History*. Breeders did indeed train both oxen and horses, using the animals' massive strength to drag their carts and plough the fields.

The 20th century saw the last of the equine labour force. The First World War, started on horseback in 1914, ended four years later to the sound of backfiring combustion engines: tireless, powerful, and no need to feed them when not in use. After the war, the factories that had built tanks assembled tractors to replace the missing farm labourers. If man and horse could plough between the rows at a rate of 0.1 hectare per hour, a tractor would be five times faster and therefore cheaper, even taking into account the cost of replacing the vines snapped by the tractor and the years of low yield from replacement plants. In total, man and horse can work 7–8 hectares of vines in a year, as against a tractor's 50 hectares.

The qualities of the animal are nevertheless obvious: beyond its environmental appeal (no machine to buy or fuel to import) and because it finds its energy locally (from pasture, cereals …), farmers particularly appreciate its agricultural virtues:

*Manolito Marti and his horse Nemo
working the Champagne Cattier vineyard*

Tillage. Although the weight under a carthorse's hoof can be greater per square centimetre than that of wide tyres at low pressure, a horse disturbs the soil less than a tractor, as demonstrated by Oronce de Beler (Burgundy, France): the tyre treads form a wall of compacted earth that obstructs earthworms and plant roots, so is detrimental to soil life and plant vitality. Engine vibration compacts the soil still more, even using a tracked vehicle. Working with a horse aerates the soil better, its consistency is noticeably finer and the vines can make the most of the *terroir*. De Beler also admires a horse's ability to work sloping ground, manoeuvre and turn around in a small space. Its intelligence and sense of balance make accidents less likely.

Gentle and precise. According to Philippe Chigard (Touraine, France), "For special, old, rugged, difficult vines, the horse is superior to the tractor. Just like *haute couture*." The powerful tractor regularly damages the trunks. The horse is gentler than the tractor and its work more sustainable, so that a grandfather can hand down to his grandson the vines he's planted, the ones that yield such high-quality juice.

A grower's contact with the vine using hand tools. De Beler designs his own tools: "You're not sitting down, or in an air-conditioned cabin, but in direct contact with the soil. In a tractor, a man loses contact with his vines."

This is confirmed by Chigard: "These tools resonate in your hands! The grower rediscovers why the vine is in trouble in one part of the plot and grows better elsewhere – pebbles, limestones, clays. What grandfather knew and we forgot."

Organic farming. Working with a horse means organic farming. "No question of spraying chemicals: horses have sensitive mucous membranes and they cough. We won't kit them out with gas masks like they did in 14/18!" laughs Chigard. "Even nettle compost can be aggressive, the horse has to be washed down afterwards." Chigard recommends spraying from a backpack wearing protective clothing.

Well-being. All agree on the pleasure to be had from the lack of engine noise and the sense of well-being offered by a horse in the vineyards, "a little paradise". The horse is a link in the trinity of man, animal and plant. Biodynamic winemaker Nicolas Joly claims that the elements within the vines enjoy the animal's presence.

How many estates use horses today? As they're sometimes used for festivities as well as regular work, it's difficult to name names. The best known is probably Château Latour, where horses are used on the 47 hectares of the mythical plot known as l'Enclos. Organic sprays are carried on the workers' backs, copper and sulphur arrive by tractor for rapid treatment if needed – so of course, the soil compaction argument is less convincing.

On the edge of the forest of Amboise, Philippe Chigard keeps seven draught horses which work in the vineyards, and trains the cart drivers. Working horses in this way also helps to ensure the survival of endangered breeds such as the Auxois, Comtois, Ardennais and Breton ...

www.cheval-vigne-vin.fr

In Burgundy, Oronce de Beler designs light hand tools intended for vineyard work.

www.equivinum.com

Horse-drawn carriage activities run by Attelage Loisirs at Plaimont (France)

Verjuice

Can late-ripening grapes be used to make wine?

Verjuice ("green juice") is a tangy liquid that was widely used in medieval cooking. It is obtained by pressing various plants (sorrel, wild fruits ...) and most often unripe grapes, especially those small clusters that are still green in autumn and that the winemakers called *verjus*. As fruit with little or no sugars (such as unripe grapes) cannot feed the yeasts that convert sugar into alcohol, it is theoretically impossible to obtain an alcoholic brew, or wine, from verjuice.

However, in the vineyards of Puglia, in southern Italy, the sun is so intense that late clusters of green grapes finally begin to ripen. Although the typical harvest normally begins in August, a second harvest in late October collects these almost sweet grapes. The winemaker takes advantage of their acidity to create fresh wines, particularly spumante.

Filippo Cassano, of Puglia's Polvanera estate, produces a sparkling rosé under the label *Metodo classico* from his Primitivo vines. Following the same method of fermentation in bottles as used for champagne, he adds 8 grams of sugar per litre to the dosage liquor, to sweeten the "*rosé brut*". One of his neighbours, Nicola Chiaromonte, also harvests again in October for verjuice.

Although the use of acidic flavours in the kitchen has greatly diminished since the Middle Ages, it lingers on in recipes such as *tête de veau vinaigrette* (slow-cooked calf's head) or in the delightful southern Italian habit of squeezing a lemon over grilled meat. Of course, in the old days cooks used only local ingredients and a great many of them didn't even know that lemons existed. Acidic juices are also used to deglaze meat pans after cooking. Sometimes mould appeared, so medieval cooks had to salt the verjuice to conserve it and discourage bacteria. The acidic taste of verjuice is nothing like that of vinegar, which is obtained after oxidation of the alcohol from wine or cider by acetic acid bacteria.

Biodynamic wine under the spotlight

What does "biodynamic" on the label signify?

The aim of any controlled or protected designation of origin (*appellation d'origine*) is a consumer guarantee that the taste of a place will be expressed in its vine and wine. But according to Nicolas Joly, a winemaker near Angers (Loire region of western France), this laudable idea has come up against four obstacles: "Herbicides kill the micro-organisms in the soil that allow the plants to feed. If I bound and gagged a guy and surrounded him with good food, he couldn't eat it. Secondly, fertilisers replace the growth linked to the soil with chemicals, which are salts. If you take in too much salt, you'll be thirsty and drink more water, which is why the growth encouraged by chemical fertilisers is mainly due to water. The third consequence of this imbalance is that the excess water causes various diseases, such as mildew or fungal infections. So pesticides that affect the whole organism were invented. The harvest is plentiful but lacks the imprint of the soil or the climate. The fourth pitfall is cellar technology, which makes up for any agricultural deficiencies without the consumer knowing. I'm thinking particularly of those terrible aromatic yeasts (there are over 300) that add a taste of citrus or blackcurrant: in short, wines that can be copied all over the world as they're deprived of their origins."

Planting new stock at Nicolas Joly's, near the Loire
The blue plastic protects the young shoots from rabbits

To address these inbuilt obstacles, Nicolas Joly has come up with the idea of biodynamic agriculture, or "dynamic biology". This approach is not new: around 1920, German agronomists who were worried about modern technology and the effect of fertilisers on soil fertility asked the advice of "anthroposophic" philosophers such as Austrian-born Rudolf Steiner, who in 1924 launched "biodynamic" farming and gave a series of lectures on agriculture. Today, the word biodynamics applies mainly to wine: combining two positive terms, it designates agricultural practices that are "in harmony with nature", thus reassuring the consumer.

Naturally, winemakers who practise biodynamics use organic farming methods: no chemical fertilisers or synthetic pesticides in the vineyard, and fermentation using fewer products than for "conventional" wine. But biodynamic winemakers also make up extraordinary "concoctions": plant infusions such as horsetail or "nettle compost" as a spray, or "horn manure" obtained by rotting dung in a cow's horn for a few months. These substances "energised" in water are used diluted to an almost homeopathic degree.

Biodynamic winemakers also respect the lunar calendar, with its "root" or "leaf" days indicated for this or that operation.

Other examples of curious practices: playing music in the vineyards and the bottling plants (see p. 110) for its supposed influence on the vines and the wine; refusing to cut the ends off the stems as other growers do when pruning, to stop foliage growth and concentrate on the grapes.

For Nicolas Joly, biodynamics is neither a list of recipes nor a fashionable marketing ploy, nor is it poetic licence. He is renowned in the wine world for having converted his vineyard of Coulée de Serrant, near Angers, to biodynamics in 1984. Since then he's travelled the world, teaching this radically different vision of agriculture.

How can a weak herbal infusion combat plant diseases?

NJ: "Conventional agriculture affects life by physical means, such as the addition of potash or nitrogen. Biodynamics works at another level: energy. Farmers know very well that their crop grows because of photosynthesis (taking water out of the equation), i.e. from the energy that the plant captures. Biodynamics favours this reception system: it doesn't act at the physical level but just before, when the plant takes in these forces and transforms them into matter."

So is the natural link disturbed?

NJ: "Yes, because thousands of satellites and antennae saturate the atmosphere. Every mobile phone, every GPS, generates frequencies that are close to cosmic, so they disorientate the system of life on Earth. It's even worse than the 50 hertz high-voltage lines because a false note is so much more disturbing when it's close to the true note."

What danger do these frequencies represent?

NJ: "Many current diseases. We're made up of vibrations: health is the balance of thousands of micro-rhythms. Imposing a dominant one disrupts them all. Young people who are born in this environment are at risk of developing health problems. This has to stop, even though there's a market for these information technologies. Depending on your genetic makeup and your diet, you'll be more or less resistant."

How should agriculture evolve?

NJ: "Agriculture will once again become the art of linking a place to the forces needed by plants and animals to best express their potential and that of their *terroir*. Add nothing, just let things happen. You'll get the true taste of a place, of a soil, that the vine captures through its roots and leaves like an antenna. Each variety will do so differently, just as three artists facing the same landscape will paint three different pictures."

How important are low yields?

NJ: "Performance is the key. Returning to what the ground is capable of yielding, there would be less disease and better quality products, at no extra cost in chemicals. Of course, it depends on your initial investment and therefore the purchase price of the vines."

What do you think of organic?

NJ: "Organic is the first step, avoiding the input of disruptive synthetic substances. We don't live on matter but on the energy it contains. When you eat chaotic and disrupted material, you too are disrupted. Organic says to nature: we respect you and you do your work. Organic is great, but unfortunately it's not enough today."

Doesn't biodynamics have a placebo effect on consumers?

NJ: "That effect is mainly on the farmer and the plants! The same treatment carried out by a bio enthusiast and someone who couldn't care less will have different effects. Like a gardener's green fingers – as yet unexplained – this placebo effect is hugely empowering to man, whose mental and emotional capacities set us above the mineral, plant and animal kingdoms. Man is the conductor. The musicians are the place, the climate, the landscape and the geology."

What are its limits?

NJ: "Biodynamic certification does not guarantee that this is reflected in the wine. In biodynamics, the results vary according to the grower's understanding and depth of commitment, like the music played by a musician or on a particular instrument. Even certification by a serious organisation like Demeter doesn't guarantee the full expression of biodynamic preparations."

How do you judge the quality of a wine?

NJ: "Open a bottle, try it, put it on one side, then try it again next day. With a conventional wine, the life fades from it. Biodynamic wine is like a young person who needs to be awakened: it explodes with life. The rush of oxygen awakens the living, but if the wine hasn't enough life in it, it dies. This also tests whether it'll keep for ten years in the cellar."

Wine from very old vines

What exactly does the reference to *Vieilles vignes* mean on some labels?

Both vine and wine, from a plant with a longevity of tens or even hundreds of years, provide one of the rare contexts where the adjective "old" is a good thing. Of course, a plant may die of disease, be infested with parasites or deliberately uprooted for a subsidy or to comply with a ban, or simply be a victim of changing fashions.

Over the years the plant develops a root system several metres long, which draws nutrients from deep within the ground. With no irrigation or fertilisers, old vines are more resistant to drought than young plants. "We don't feed it; it'll fend for itself!" jokes Ales Kristančič of the Movia estate in Slovenia. Although the harvest is less abundant with age, the grapes and the wines from old vines are naturally richer in minerals drawn from the soil.

How do you recognise an "old vine"? This indication is of value on the label, but its use is up to the producer – some apply it to plants that are only twenty or thirty years old. Although the age of a rootstock can be estimated by the look of it, the growers, their parents or neighbours, generally know when their plots were planted. The winery's records may also keep track. More remote or undocumented times leave matters open to interpretation – in Europe, an old non-grafted vine probably dates from before the phylloxera crisis of the 1860s.

Centennial vines growing up a poplar, Caputo estate, Aversa (Italy)

Some examples of very old vines:

In France, the garden at Sarragachies (Gers), included in the French Inventory of Historic Monuments (see p. 78), dates back to 1820. The photos opposite show owners Jean-Pascal Pédebernade and his father René among their vines.

Plaimont Producteurs also make wine from grapes of another notable grafted vine dating from around 1880. Its plantation marks the rebirth of an entire vineyard after phylloxera and reflects a key period in French viticulture. The vine grows near the Porche de la Madeleine, a 14th-century building, hence its name *Madeleine de Saint-Mont* with a nod to Proust. The ancient roots in the clay-gravel soil give this wine its structure and complexity.

In the Cour-Cheverny appellation zone of the Loire valley, a plot of the Romorantin B grape variety belonging to Henri Marionnet dates back to 1850.

In Champagne, Bollinger Vieilles produces its *Vieilles vignes françaises* vintage from own-root (ungrafted) vines untouched by phylloxera.

In Portugal's Douro valley, the La Nacional plot also escaped the insect and being uprooted. The vintage port *Noval nacional* is the result.

Castel Katzenzungen, in Trentino-Alto Adige (Italy), has a vine that is over 350 years old; its grapes produce an acidic white wine known as *Versoaln*.

The oldest vine still alive in Europe is thought to have been planted 400 years ago at Maribor (Slovenia) and still yields a few bottles of wine.

The oldest plant ever identified by botanists is a Tasmanian shrub, known as King's Holly, at 43,000 years old; like the vine, it is adept at putting out shoots and taking over a space.

Tasmanian King's Holly (*Lomatia tasmanica*): see A. J. J. Lynch et al., 1998, Genetic evidence that *Lomatia tasmanica* (Proteaceae) is an ancient clone, *Australian Journal of Botany*, 46.

Jack and the beanstalk vines

These 15-metre vines attach themselves to poplar trees, as they have done since antiquity

Vines are creepers that naturally grow up towards the sun. As Pliny the Elder explains in his *Natural History*, the Romans let them climb trees, which cut out the need to install stakes while distancing the grapes from the humidity and predators at ground level.

Of course, harvesting in the treetops was risky and the workers stipulated that, if they fell, they would be "burned and buried at the owner's expense".

In his 1600 work *The Theatre of Agriculture and Husbandry Fields*, Olivier de Serres also describes vines clinging to tall trees: "These vines *en hautain* (at great height) were developed in France mainly in Brie, Champagne, Burgundy, Berry and other provinces," i.e. mainly in the north, where sunshine is sometimes lacking and humidity is high.

Today, a few particularly high vines persist in Italy, Crete and Portugal. Those of the celebrated *vinho verde* grow along the roadsides and in gardens. Between the rows, which were about 15 metres apart, the farmers grew wheat, hemp or vegetables, a combination of different species that is known as interplanting (see p. 96). This ancient method of cultivation, which uses little ground space but is labour intensive, has almost completely disappeared.

Portuguese *vinho verde* now uses trellised vines so that the training and harvesting are easier to mechanise.

In Campania (Italy), some estates still make wine from hundred-year-old non-grafted vines that have resisted phylloxera. This rootstock of the white Asprinio ("bitter") grape climbs poplars because the tree grows fast, straight up towards the light, and its small leaves let the vine take advantage of the sunshine. Another height-related advantage: the wind from the nearby Mediterranean dries out any moisture and prevents the grapes from developing fungal diseases.

Carlo Numeroso, owner of the Borboni estate, has some of these giant vines near Aversa (Campania). As they stand almost 15 metres tall, they're neither pruned nor treated. To harvest these spectacular green walls laden with grapes, the workers climb ladders (each has their own, adapted to their size and shape) and fill small pointed baskets called *fascine*, which sink into the ground when dropped. An assistant empties out the grapes and the baskets are pulled up again by rope, like groceries in Naples. "But young people no longer want to work this way," you'll hear. "My youngest picker is 60," sighs Mario Caputo, another winemaker.

Each vine yields a large quantity of not very ripe grapes that are still acidic – characteristic of the Asprinio d'Aversa appellation. Several wineries make good use of this acidity, producing a sparkling wine by the traditional (champagne) bottled method or in a classic closed tank.

Paradoxically, Numeroso also turns this variety of grape into its polar opposite – dessert wine. To achieve this curiosity, he harvests in October, dries the grapes under cover and presses them in January: "I wanted to bring back a childhood memory. After the harvest, my parents kept a few branches and we ate grapes at Christmas. They also pressed them to make a sweet wine."

Unconventional fermentation methods

*"Wine is proof of existence,
Not of God, but of the existence of man!"
Don Pasta, Pantelleria*

Since Palaeolithic times people have enjoyed the tiny grapes of the wild vine *Vitis sylvestris*, as borne out by the 500,000-year-old seeds that archaeologists have found at Mediterranean digs. Traces of tartaric acid on pottery from the Hajji Firuz Tepe site (Iran) show that grapes had been fermented there since the 6th millennium BC. The Greek and Roman empires perfected winemaking, which is as much art as technique, according to winemakers from the Puglia region of south-east Italy: "We'll show you an interpretation, a 'reading' of Primitivo" (a local grape variety). Indeed, like a concert or a play, any vintage is an interpretation.

Vinification is the process of converting grapes into wine. The principle is simple: for white wine, press the grapes, save the juice, ferment it with added yeast or let it ferment naturally. For red wine, crush the berries so that most of them split, add yeast or not, and let them macerate and ferment for a few days or weeks with their dark skins, then press them. To sum up: for white, press then ferment. The opposite for red: ferment then press. Rosé is treated almost like a red, but is macerated for only a few hours to reach the required coloration — just as tea darkens as it infuses.

Cryomaceration with dry ice in a Quintessence barrel

The vat lifter at Ca' del Bosco (Franciacorta, Italian sparkling wine) avoids disturbing the wine by having to pump it

Symbolically, man destroys his work, treading the grapes and allowing them to spoil and be transformed – it's the myth of the Resurrection, a bet never won in advance. Fermentation is always a delicate operation. Hence Judaism, which is closely observant of the concepts of pure and impure, has made recommendations as to what constitutes kosher wine. In Islam there is an outright ban on fermented beverages.

Some definitions:

The oenologist is a wine doctor, a master technician who, after sample analyses (of sugar, alcohol, acidity ...), advises on the addition of a particular yeast, cooling the tanks to a certain temperature to slow the fermentation, or reheating them to restart it. All biochemical phenomena depend on temperature. In other words, the oenologist is a sommelier, a wine consultant and a taster who is knowledgeable about wine and can give advice on matching it with food. So there's a difference between the oenologist-agronomist and the oenologist-taster.

Organic wine is made with grapes from organic farming, according to Europe-wide legislation and overseen by a certification agency.

As winemaking enterprises vary in size, they are divided into industrial organic and artisanal organic. The first has a wide distribution of large quantities of a product of standard quality and taste. The artisanal sector allows variations in taste, by year and by blend.

And natural wine? The word "natural" gives rise to debate among some winemakers, who comment ironically: "Wine is cultural, religious, human ... anything but natural! You'll never find it in nature, except perhaps in sweet grape juice that hasn't fermented yet. Wine doesn't make itself, so there's no such thing as natural wine. Natural wine is called vinegar!" Sometimes, so-called natural wines give off a slightly volatile or acetic acidity (just like the vinegar family, which is pleasant in small doses), which adds a certain freshness and accentuates the flavours.

Of course wine is cultural, because it was invented by humans. Applied to wine, the adjective "natural" describes a wine with minimal inputs and interventions. This type of wine, said to be non-yeasty, doesn't use cultured commercial yeasts that can add a particular taste to the wine. So the winemaker lets natural yeasts in the atmosphere and on the berries take their course, while keeping a close eye on operations.

This is how, a week before the harvest, Frank Cornelissen (Sicily) manages his yeast trials:

"I pick 40 kilos of grapes in the vineyard and destem them. I press them, then they ferment alone. If the result is good and the flavours are perfect, I use this to trigger the large-scale fermentation for the entire harvest. If it's bad, I throw it out and try again."

In this way he uses indigenous yeasts typical of his Mount Etna *terroir*, but which he has selected. "Be warned: rather than make natural wine, you must make a wine that's good and true! And very clean, so it keeps without the addition of sulphites."

Biodynamics sees the Earth as a living being connected to the cosmos. In the vineyard and in the cellar, these winemakers work with their vines and wines according to the phases of the moon. They sometimes use oval fermentation vessels, such as amphorae, or egg-shaped tanks such as the one at Moulin de Pouzy (Bergerac, France), which encourages the movement of the wine during fermentation. But biodynamic producers aren't the only ones to use ovoid amphorae and tanks.

The best shape for a fermentation tank is the subject of lengthy debate: the terracotta amphora is the oldest type. The Celts, using the oak from their forests and their iron tools, successfully constructed leak-proof barrels. Today, few winemakers use barrels for vinification inside — although they seem to be catching on again for high-end wines. On the other hand, barrels are used for the slow maturation of the wine known as élevage ("raising" with care and attention: see p. 222).

Stainless-steel tanks are easier to clean than wood and their temperature can be regulated like a refrigerator, with heat exchangers dipped into the fermenting grape juice (must). Others have thermo-regulated walls. Temperature control is essential during fermentation. The cheaper concrete vats are valued for their thermal inertia.

During the fermentation of red wine, the crushed berries rise to the surface and form a cap, which has to be regularly submerged in the must to make way for a new layer that can be oxygenated. *Remontage* (drawing off the must near the bottom and pumping it back over the top) and *pigeage** (pressing it down with a stick) help to achieve a homogeneous mix. Once fermentation ceases, the wine is kept in a closed container, away from oxygen. The operation known as *ullage*** fills the barrels to the brim, so that the wine can't oxidise.

Of course, as in any recipe, the operator's skill intervenes; with the same basic ingredients, the dish will be different depending on the cook. In the obscurity of the cellar, the dark surface of the wine reflects the personality of the winemaker.

*French term for stamping grapes in an open area or fermentation tanks.
**From the French word *ouillage*, which refers to the evaporation of wine from a barrel. The headspace left in a container is the "ullage" or "ullage space".

Wines with little or no alcohol

A weakness has become a prized virtue

So-called "table" wine, long considered as a food, was sold by alcohol strength by volume, 12 per cent being more highly valued than 11 per cent. A high alcohol content meant better conservation and more powerful aromas: the alcohol is both a conserving agent and the vehicle and enhancer of flavours … not to mention intoxicating.

The International Organisation of Vine and Wine (OIV) specifications are that "the acquired alcoholic strength should not be less than 8.5 per cent" or 7 per cent for rare appellations.

Some OIV member countries would like the word "wine" to apply to non-alcoholic beverages also, particularly for exports to Muslim countries with high purchasing power that ban alcohol or tax it heavily. Other members counter that such drinks couldn't be referred to as "wine".

Another good reason to develop low-alcohol wines is because of the fiscal policies of northern European countries (Norway, Sweden, United Kingdom …) which tax imports by alcoholic strength. Grapes are increasingly ripe and sweet thanks to global warming. Mastery of alcoholic strength is now crucial.

Winemakers are well aware of this trend. Some put a lower strength on the label than is actually the case to reassure customers, as a tolerance of plus or minus 0.5 per cent is allowed.

Others add spring water to too-sweet musts before fermentation, to reduce the potential alcohol: a harmless additive but nevertheless illegal because of fraud and watered-down wine precedents … and detectable if treated tap water is used. Still other growers harvest in the early morning, mechanically, as the dew can reduce alcohol level by 0.5 per cent.

The Ribeyrenc grape has a low alcohol yield

To limit the alcohol content, the simplest method is to interrupt fermentation before all the sugars have been converted. These "residual" sugars bring sweetness and a pleasant fruitiness. Some wines made by this method are described below:

Blanquette de Limoux. Because of the method, known locally as *ancestrale* or *rurale* (or *gaillacoise* in the Gaillac region of south-west France), this is considered to be the world's oldest sparkling wine. It involves stopping the white Mauzac grape fermenting by extraction and filtration. The partially fermented must is bottled and the cellar temperature raised to restart the fermentation process. Carbon dioxide is released, giving the wine its effervescence. The AOC *Limoux méthode ancestrale* yields only 6–7 per cent alcohol.

www.limoux-aoc.com

Cerdon from AOC Bugey (photo p. 155) is a sparkling rosé from Savoie (Rhône-Alpes region). The red Gamay grape is pressed soon after harvest and its pink juice ferments along with its natural yeasts. After filtration the wine is bottled, when a second fermentation takes place, effervescing until it reaches approximately 8 per cent alcohol. The non-converted sugars give it a mellow taste.

www.vinsdubugey.net

In Italy, Asti spumante is another sparkling wine with low alcohol content (7–9 per cent); it's sweet because part of the sugar is unfermented. But the entire process takes place in stainless-steel tanks rather than in bottles, which makes the wine easier to transport and avoids yeast deposits.

www.astidocg.info

Fermentation can also be interrupted to produce a still wine, such as Vignerons de Buzet's *Nuage* (9 per cent alcohol), in rosé or white vintages, in which fermentation of the Merlot grape is interrupted before the yeasts have converted all the sugars. Further fermentation is prevented by filtering to remove the yeasts followed by a light sulphiting. So no bubbles.

www.vignerons-buzet.fr

Some forgotten varieties (see p. 88) also offer low-alcohol possibilities. Thierry Navarre found a few plants on his Languedoc estate from the red Ribeyrenc grape that produces fruity, light wines, even under the intense sun of the south of France. This variety is not currently registered on the International List of Vine Varieties and no clone is authorised, although action is being taken to safeguard it. Nonconventional hybrids with no appellation, known as PIWI varieties (see p. 100), can also produce wines that are low in alcohol.

At La Colombette estate, father and son François and Vincent Pugibet are experimenting with these PIWI disease-resistant grape varieties. From classic grapes (Grenache, Syrah, Chardonnay), they produce the *Plume* range, which is a great success at 9 per cent: "Our goal is for people to take pleasure in drinking – and finishing – the bottle. Alcohol is needed to conserve the wine, but often masks its faults."

www.lacolombette.fr

Formulating a totally alcohol-free "wine" can be done by means other than fermentation. Thus, in a fun presentation and with a nod to champagne, Champomy® for children is apple juice with added carbon dioxide, full of festive bubbles like soda.

Most alcohol-free wines have been fermented and dealcoholised by a method such as reverse osmosis. The Oenodia company specialises in subtractive techniques that separate the components of the wine, using filtering membranes and ion exchange induced by an electrical field. Subtracting instead of adding (additives are increasingly controversial) is an intellectually stimulating, modern technology.

www.oenodia.com

The *Night orient* range (0.0 per cent alcohol) is made in Belgium from Spanish grapes, using a method mid-way between that used for grape juice and alcohol-free wine. The white comes from Chardonnay, the red from Merlot, the bubbles from "concentrated musts", and the final product benefits from the halal certification that allows Muslims to drink it. The message is communicated through constant visual references to wine, without ever using the word.

www.nightorient.com

The strongest wine in the world

Superprimitivo, produced under the sun of the Ionian Sea, is notable for its extraordinary alcohol level of 19.5 per cent

The juice of ripe grapes contains sugars that feed the yeasts (fungal spores naturally present on the leaves and in the cellar that will cause fermentation), which release alcohol and carbon dioxide. Their feast ends when there's no more sugar to consume, or if the strength of the alcohol kills the yeasts themselves: about 18 per cent appears to be the maximum level they can survive.

For this reason, wines over 18 per cent are usually obtained by adding distilled alcohol, during or after fermentation: these are called fortified wines. Note that there is no upper limit to the level of alcohol in wine (Guido Baldeschi, Oenology Commission, International Organisation of Vine and Wine).

There are rare exceptions, however. In the southern Italian region of Puglia, where the sun beats down relentlessly, the Primitivo grape (the name means "early") matures quickly: harvest begins in late August. If delayed, the sugars concentrate in the overripe grapes and the yeasts feast. Nicola Chiaromonte, a grower at Acquaviva delle Fonti, sells his classic vintage *Muro Sant'Angelo* at 16 per cent and his reserve at 17 per cent. These alcohol levels are not uncommon and are sometimes found in the appellation zone with its 10,000 hectares of Primitivo: the *Mille e uno*, for example, at 18.5 per cent. But Chiaromonte has already beaten the record with his outstanding *Superprimitivo* at 19.5 per cent. "Next year, we'll bring one out at 20 per cent!" he says.

A Primitivo plantation on Nicola Chiaromonte's estate

The biological activity of yeast continues at such high levels of alcohol because there are "local yeasts that can convert sugar in these extreme conditions".

In fact, the yeasts don't consume all the sugar: 5–10 grams per litre remain after fermentation, which rounds out the flavours in the style of New World wines. A few months after the harvest, these wines are ready to drink and give off notes of black fruits, preserved plums, cherries in eau-de-vie, dried figs, carob, liquorice, tobacco, chocolate and jam … while keeping the vivacity and freshness of their youth.

High alcohol levels: pros and cons

Competition judges tend to reward expressive wines, whether for their aroma or their flavour. Alcohol tends to lift the taste. The US wine critic Robert Parker's ratings on a 100-point scale favour wines with high alcohol content, a style that's been followed by winemakers worldwide.

In France too, in the southern vineyards of Rhône and Languedoc, the alcohol level is high: whereas there used to be a market for large quantities of wine, now quality wines in smaller quantities are sought after. So winemakers limit their output, carrying out a green harvest in June to eliminate some of the grape clusters so that the remainder can benefit from all the sap of the vine and reach perfect maturity. Thanks to localised, very accurate online weather forecasts, growers are harvesting later, so the grapes are riper.

Climate change is also playing a role in increased alcohol levels. The limits are both fiscal and psychological. Nicola Chiaromonte exports his wines from Puglia to Asia and the USA, but not to the UK or Sweden where alcohol is heavily taxed. A number of restaurant customers are concerned about drinking wine at 14.5 per cent and prefer to order 13 per cent, even if the difference seems insignificant.

Iraq's clandestine wines

In Kurdistan, a few growers discreetly strive to cultivate vines and make wine

Is viniculture disappearing from the land of Mesopotamia, where it was developed? Paradoxically, it isn't Islam that destroyed the wine industry in Iraq, but Saddam Hussein, a secular wine lover whose taste for *Mateus*, a sparkling Portuguese rosé found in the cellars of his palace, was well known. The genocide he perpetrated in Kurdistan from 1987 to 1991 and the ensuing population exodus meant that the vineyards were abandoned.

The terrorism born of war is now sufficiently menacing to force growers underground. Discretion is the rule when it comes to alcoholic beverages. With no promotion and no phylloxera, local varieties and wild vines cling to the hillsides. The presence of well-maintained rootstock and plots that have been recently planted with prunings suggests that the growers are resisting – second nature to the Kurds.

The grape varieties sold in Kurdistan's markets or by the roadside are black (Mermerk, Rosh Mew), red (Taefi, Kamali), yellow (Zarek, Hejaze, Khateni, Keshmesh) or red and white (Helwani). "With these grapes, we can do anything," explains a stallholder. "Table grapes, raisins, juice, wine, arak, vinegar!" The conversation naturally veers towards the fermentation process. "Here, twenty-five years before Saddam Hussein flattened the villages, we made wine and arak." And now? "We still do it!" exclaims a neighbour.

In a Christian village near Amadiya, the vines grow vigorously around the church to form hedges and pergolas. A thick non-grafted root, 30 centimetres in diameter, feeds a vast canopy of leaves and clusters of grapes. Its owner describes the production of arak: "I harvest the grapes, crush them and leave them in a tank for seven days before distilling to get a grape alcohol of about 70 degrees." He responds to a request to visit his set-up with a smile: "We haven't made any for years!"

At the corner shop, a man sipping tea with friends sells his own wine in recycled bottles: "€7 for the good one, less for the other." This fruity wine, fermented a few weeks earlier, is already oxidised. "I crush Mermek grapes in a vat. After seven days of fermentation, I bottle the juice. I produce a few hundred bottles a year." His childhood memories are of villagers making their wine in earthenware jars. He says he bought a still in Baghdad but now it's nowhere to be seen. "It's in a nearby village; anyway we don't use it much any more …". He too refers to himself as an "Assyrian Christian".

The bishop of Dohuk, Monsignor Rabban, opened a secular free school for boys and girls, both Muslims and Christians. This even-handed diplomat, respected by all, refuses to reveal the source of communion wine in his diocese, presumably to protect his winemaker friends. The secret is as well guarded as if it had been heard in the confessional.

In the mountains near the Turkish border, a church supplier agrees to testify on condition that his name isn't mentioned and no pictures taken in which he might be recognised.

His village is sited near the snowy peaks where several hundred thousand Kurds fled during the winter of 1991; no house was left standing after the passage of Saddam Hussein's troops, as in almost all of Kurdistan. Now, the people are rebuilding with reinforced concrete and the vines are growing again, spilling over the walls of the Christian cemetery beside the church, forming hedges and invading the village, a witness to the intense wine-producing activities of the past. Rainfall is 800–1,000 millimetres a year, altitude 800 metres, with brilliant sunshine.

The anonymous winemaker describes his method of preparing several hundred bottles a year in the family washroom: "Pick the grapes and transport them in crates. Don't wash them because the chlorinated water affects the fermentation. Wearing clean boots, crush them in a basin. Let them ferment with natural yeasts. Transfer them to a demijohn, filling the neck with straw to let the carbon dioxide escape without oxygen getting in. Let it settle, then siphon it off." He obtains a wine that is between 9 and 12 per cent. For his rosé, he mixes red and white grapes. Before the massacres, his father and grandfather made wine in jars in the local tradition. This amateur winemaker – who holds a doctorate in petrochemicals – distils arak with five passes through the still and some complex purification processes. He then adds aniseed from his garden. "There is no Kurdish wine – just Kurds who make wine," he jokes, "but they're unaware of the chemical processes."

Kurdistan is still a treasure trove of biodiversity and pre-phylloxera vines. Although the future of Kurdish wine seems uncertain, the world's viticultural future will perhaps lie in this fabulous gene bank: the vines of Mesopotamia, where Nebuchadnezzar II (c. 604–562 BC) was king.

Rare sweet wines

What techniques are used to produce a sweet wine?
Any exceptions?

"So when do you add the sugar?" a customer sometimes asks an appalled winemaker: "No, we never sweeten the wine – sometimes we just add sugar to the must to increase the final alcohol content, a technique known as chaptalisation." The winemakers of Champagne also add a little sugar to the bottle before the second fermentation and expedition.

In theory, wine is never sweetened. However, there are some exceptions: mulled wine, drunk in winter; certain flavoured wines (such as grapefruit rosé, which has added grapefruit juice or flavouring, sweetened with grenadine); and the historic beverage hypocras to which, since antiquity, honey has been added to make the wine drinkable … despite its downsides such as a vinegary taste, oxidation, and maderisation (turning brown like madeira). The resulting liquid was named hypocras in honour of Hippocrates (the ancient Greek physician considered to be the "father" of medicine) because of the medicinal and aphrodisiac properties attributed to it. The Crusaders brought the recipe back from the East. Hypocras is still manufactured today – white, rosé or red, depending on the base wine used – and is drunk cold. A variant of hypocras, *Garhiofilatum*, a white wine flavoured with cloves and other spices, is made near Montpellier in the south of France.

Two techniques are traditionally accepted for making sweet wines. The first is to stop the grape juice fermenting by adding wine alcohol before the yeasts consume all the sugar, or even before fermentation starts. This liqueur is known by several names: *mistelle* (from the Italian *misto*, "mixture"), fortified wine, dessert wine or *vin doux naturel* (VDN).

Passerillage of grapes at Coffele (Soave, Italy)

Alcohol conserves, as fruit is preserved in eau-de-vie, but in smaller amounts: the final level is between 15 and 22 per cent alcohol. The best-known wines of this type are port, madeira, Maury, Banyuls, etc., but there are others such as red or white (*doré*) Rasteau. These two wines from the Rhone valley are derived from the Grenache Noir grape with its white juice, harvested when very ripe. Fermentation is halted by the addition of vinous alcohol (from other distilled wines). Ageing takes place in oak barrels and vats. The Rasteau rouge exudes aromas of cherry, cocoa, spices; the Rasteau doré, dried fruit, honey, quince, apricot …

On the Italian island of Pantelleria, the sweet wine known as Passito liquoroso is three times cheaper than *Passito di Pantelleria* (see p. 119). It is simply a liqueur wine, obtained by pouring alcohol over the grape juice.

Crimea Kagor is a remarkable wine in several ways. The red grapes are destemmed, crushed and heated to extract intense colour and tannins. Fermentation stops when alcohol is poured over the must. Ukrainian before 2014 and Russian since annexation, this sweet red wine was meant to be a copy of Cahors, hence its name. The best known comes from the Massandra winery.

The second technique for making sweet wine is to use very ripe grapes, with residual sugars after fermentation (wine from raisined grapes, straw wine …).

Some examples:

Quebec ice wine (*vin de glace*) dried on the vine (see p. 36).

Jura straw wine (*vin de paille*).

Pacherenc du Vic-Bihl, from Plaimont, also dried on the vine, so nets have to be used to keep the birds off (see p. 120).

Passito di Pantelleria, dried on the ground and vinified in an unusual way (see p. 119).

Sulphite-free vat in the cellars of Prince Spadafora (Sicily)

In conventional wine production, the legal limit of SO_2 is 150 milligrams/litre (red) or 200 mg/l (white and rosé). Sweet wines can receive up to 400 mg/l of SO_2. For "organic" wine, the dose is reduced even if the law plays safe: the SO_2 shouldn't exceed 100 mg/l for dry red wines and 150 mg/l for dry whites and rosés. Other wines must have a dose lower than 30 mg/l as far as the current regulations go.

Although these doses of SO_2 are significantly lower than the amount added to dried fruit, especially apricots, they can cause digestive problems. At high doses, the wine takes on a sulphurous smell like matches. But banning sulphites outright is risky: if the bottles aren't transported and stored in cool conditions, the wine may develop an unpleasant taste or start fermenting again and explode.

All winemakers have their own ideas on how to limit potential damage. Frank Cornelissen (Sicily): "I don't treat the vines because I want them to defend themselves. Likewise I want my wines to defend themselves; and for a wine to hold its own without sulphites, it must have good concentration and good minerality."

Bordeaux winemakers OenoTeam follow this strategy: "Not replacing sulphites seemed risky to us. So we fill the biological environment with known micro-organisms that deter the unwanted ones. This bioprotection principle avoids the use of SO_2 in winemaking, while monitoring the aromatic variations. The benefits are pure and fruity wines. When fermentation ends, sulphiting is carried out, but the total SO_2 is still very low."

Several estates are testing OenoTeam's bioprotection techniques: Château de Cérons (Graves), Château La Grave Figeac and Château Haut-Veyrac (Saint-Émilion grand cru), Château Grand Français (Bordeaux supérieur), Domaine de Moulin Pouzy (Bergerac), Château de Payre (Côtes de Bordeaux), Château Bélingard (Bergerac) and Château du Bousquet (Côtes de Bourg).

Why is white wine said to cause headaches?

The poor reputation of white wine, especially medium-sweet, comes from the SO_2 dose required to ensure the proper conservation of a liquid rich in residual sugars. In the presence of both sugar and yeast, fermentation may resume. A dry wine (whether red or white) or one with a high alcohol level will keep better than a sweet or light wine.

Paradoxically, a liqueur or a very sweet wine requires fewer sulphites because at high dose the sugar itself is a preservative, as in jam-making.

In the early 20th century, the sulphite level was higher because consumers enjoyed sweet-tasting wines, particularly champagne. And the health hazards of sulphites were unknown.

Why the mention "contains sulphites" on a wine label that claims "no added sulphites"?

Because fermentation produces sulphites naturally. Even though the winemaker doesn't add any, they're there in the wine.

Coolness and filtering control are key to reducing sulphite levels

The amphora wines of Georgia

Wines in giant amphorae have retained the flavours of antiquity

Georgia, with Russia to the north and Turkey to the south, has seen many waves of invaders over the centuries. So the farmers of this fertile land, with its temperate climate, have long been in the habit of hiding their wine, oil and cereals in amphorae, buried out of sight. Examples of this pottery, known as *kvevri* ("large jar"), containing an orange wine that is still drinkable despite its acidity and slightly vinegary taste, are sometimes excavated.

Under communism, Georgia's wine-producing reputation led to the construction of manufacturing plants whose wine was exported throughout the Soviet empire. But rural and townspeople alike continued to harvest the vines from their gardens and prepare their family wine in amphorae.

The recipe is simple, as explained by grower Tamasi Natroshvili: "We tread the grape clusters, then put them to ferment in amphorae. We stir the mix with a stick. After twenty to twenty-five days, when the marc (skins and stem) has sunk to the bottom, we transfer the wine to another amphora. A wicker basket is used as a filter. We distil the marc and the small stems to obtain an alcohol called *tchatcha*. Two weeks later, we transfer the wine to yet another amphora and cork it tightly. Three decantings follow: in spring; for the Transfiguration of Christ festival (6 August); and for the new harvests. For successful storage the amphorae must always be full of wine."

Amphorae unearthed

This *kakhetian* method (named after Georgia's premier wine-producing region of Kakheti, pronounced *careti*) requires no running water, electricity, barrels, temperature control or winepress: just a stick, a basket and some amphorae.

The wines made by the *imerouli* method (from the Imereti region) are less harsh because the grapes are hand-separated from the stems that would spoil the taste. The winemaking process is identical for both red and white grapes. It's also a fascinating journey back in time, throwing light on the methods of antiquity.

Today, this ancient and rustic wine, with its marked acidity, is popular with lovers of natural wine, and cellars with buried amphorae are being built.

Unfortunately it's difficult to find potters to make these vessels, which can contain from 1 to 3 tonnes of wine. The ancient amphorae are porous, dirty and often damaged, so restoring them is difficult.

Where can Georgian amphorae wines be found?

Several wines produced in Georgia are fermented in amphorae: *Clos des amandiers*, *Our Wine*, from Soliko Tsaishvili, Zurab Topuridze and Iago Bitarishvili.
www.triplea.it

Amphorae buried up to their necks, out of sight and out of mind

Vegetarian wine

Vines aren't animals, so why speak of vegetarian wine?

Wine is pure fermented grape juice with no added colours or flavours. However, winemakers are free to use various methods to clean the grapes, control the fermentation, preserve, clarify and acidify the wine … The International Organisation of Vine and Wine website lists the products authorised by the International Oenological Codex. The most conventional additions are:

Sugar before fermentation if the crop doesn't contain enough naturally (chaptalisation).

Yeasts that define the style of the wine. The famous "banana" flavour of some new wines comes from the use of these yeasts. They aren't artificial aromas but natural yeasts selected and reproduced in the laboratory; sometimes genetically modified, certainly less natural, even if "the use of genetically modified bacteria will be submitted to prior authorisation of competent authorities" in each country, according to the OIV.

According to centuries-old natural techniques, winemakers have added proteins to clarify the wine, i.e. to avoid deposits in the bottle and cloudiness in the glass: egg white, ox blood, fish glue, pork gelatin and milk casein have all been used. Even if the addition is at a homeopathic dose (three egg whites to a 225 litre barrel, or 0.0004 per cent of total volume), it worries those with allergies.

Harvest in Savoie (France)

Wine-filtering machine

The food crises of recent years have called into question these centuries-old techniques. For example, mad cow disease led to the prohibition of ox blood and the European Union now stipulates that allergens such as albumin must be reported, as for any foodstuff.

Winemakers are wary of misunderstandings should the public discover on the label that in addition to sulphites, the wine contains milk, pork, eggs ... especially as exports to countries such as India and the new vegan trend look for wine that is free from animal by-products, for both religious and philosophical reasons.

Some winemakers, especially fans of "natural wines", have decided to turn this obstacle into an advantage and stress that their wine is "neither yeasted nor filtered", hence its rather cloudy aspect. Frédéric Brochet, for example, of the organic Ampelidae winery (Loire valley, France) was the first to certify his wines through the UK-based Vegan Society.

Others have abandoned the old ways of clarifying and brightening their wine in favour of more modern, chemical or physical processes, such as filters, bentonite (absorbent clay) or diatoms (algae). They could all claim: "During the making of this wine, no animals have been killed or exploited," but few of them do so ...

A speciality Bordelais pastry known as *canelé* has been invented to make use of the mountains of egg yolk remaining after the whites have been used to clarify wine.

Champagne, an English invention?

In the Middle Ages, monks all over France cultivated vines and made wine from the grapes to celebrate the Eucharist, but also for sale. The climate of Champagne is colder than that of the Burgundian abbeys, but the same grape varieties – Pinot Noir and Chardonnay – were chosen. To facilitate trade and move the barrels, the vines were astutely planted near waterways (Marne, Aube, Aisne) with their confluence at Paris and Rouen. From 816 to 1825, the coronation of thirty-three kings of France at Reims meant unparalleled prestige for the local wine, even though the grapes didn't always ripen and the wine from some vineyards turned out rather acidic.

From their neighbours in Champagne, the English bought barrels of this wine: it was normally still, without bubbles, and with added sugar cane to soften the acidity.

Pierre Pérignon, known as Dom Pérignon, a Benedictine monk (1639–1715), observed a mysterious phenomenon that only the work of Louis Pasteur (1822–1895), who revealed the action of yeasts, was able to explain: with the cold of winter the activity of the micro-organisms in the barrels stops, only to restart when the temperature rises. The addition of sugar feeds the yeasts and activates them. If the wine is already bottled, the bottles will explode: they are unable to withstand the pressure exerted by the carbon dioxide from this new fermentation.

A tasting session at Mumm champagne

Mumm pupitre wine rack

The pragmatic English could produce stronger glass thanks to the high temperatures achieved from burning coal, while the French were still heating their foundries with wood. For these reasons (added sugar and resistant bottles), several writers maintain that champagne is an English rather than a French invention.

The method of making champagne remains unchanged: the first fermentation in an open tank gives a still wine, the second is carried out in solid bottles with the addition of sugar beet* (*liqueur de tirage*).** The bottles are closed with a crown cap, like a beer bottle, and the second fermentation begins. The carbon dioxide can't escape and forms bubbles in the wine.

To remove the unsightly dead yeast or lees, the bottles are stacked on a rack and gradually inclined so that the sediment falls towards the neck. The process known as disgorgement involves opening each bottle to eliminate this deposit and then nimbly topping up the level with *liqueur d'expédition*. ***

Whether from beet or cane, the sugar added to launch the second fermentation is sucrose (chemical formula $C_{12}H_{22}O_{11}$). For one of his blends, winemaker Fabrice Pouillon use $C_6H_{22}O_6$, sugar from very ripe grape juice of the same plot and the same vintage. So his champagne is entirely local, with no external ingredients. The blend is known as *Chemin de bois*.

*Sugar beet was developed in 1811 by Benjamin Delessert, to overcome the blockade of West Indian sugar imposed by the English at war with Napoleon.

**A syrupy mixture of wine, sugar and yeast added to cause a secondary fermentation that induces carbonation.

***A mixture of wine and sugar added to balance the acidity or to give the wine a degree of sweetness, if required.

> ### Belgian version of champagne
> Over the border in Belgium, Ruffus sparking wines use the same grape varieties (Chardonnay, Pinot Noir, Pinot Meunier) and the same traditional method as champagne, but with only a twelve-month ageing period (fifteen months for champagne).

Bordeaux made with dry ice

An innovative technique that is spectacularly chemical-free

No chemicals and entirely natural: the thick cloud that emanates from the barrel is only liquid carbon dioxide, the CO_2 in the air we breathe. On the Côtes de Bourg, near Bordeaux (France), Stéphane Destrade uses dry ice to macerate part of his *Château de Blissa* harvest in order to keep the fruit fresh. This technique, which is extremely rare in Bordeaux, has been spotted by Sophie Pallas and her team who select unusual bottles, forgotten varieties and ancient techniques, as well as the "innovations" of creative oenologists, for Autrement Vins (www.autrementvin.com).

How it's done: Destrade first leaves his grapes for a classic cold soak (cryomaceration) in new oak barrels at a temperature of 6 °C for six days. Every six hours, dry ice is added so that the temperature remains low. The grapes soak in the cold for a few days before fermentation, hence the name of the method. Cryomaceration, which is often used for white wines, gives more fruity aromas than if the fermentation had begun at room temperature straight after harvesting – just as a casserole stewed slowly at low temperature will taste better than one using a pressure cooker.

Of course, this method is expensive in storage space and electricity for cooling (here with dry ice): respect for fruity, delicate aromas comes at a price.

Six days after the harvest, Destrade pours another measure of dry ice (liquid carbon dioxide at −78.5 °C) over the grapes. An impressive white cloud rises from the barrel and the berries burst. "This process gives mellower tannins and sexier wines," comments Stéphane Toutoundji, oenologist at Blissa. "The balance is more interesting, the wines more colourful and fruity. The ice is like a sorbet, extracting the best from the fruit."

Another advantage is that carbon dioxide saturation displaces oxygen around the grapes, preventing damage from oxidation.

During the six days of fermentation at 18 °C, the mixture of berries, juice and skin is stirred with a stick (an operation called *pigeage*) and the must is pumped up (*remontage*) so that fermentation and colour is homogeneous (see p. 153).

As in making tea, the more the mixture is stirred, the stronger it gets; and the more material extracted, the more tannic and colourful the juice.

The wine is then set aside while the Quintessence cooper refits the lids of the barrels in which the wine will age.

Destrade was a London banker who left everything to take over the family property and create a wine that pleases him: "fruity, very fresh and pure, with silky tannins".

A new-generation wine, rare in traditional Bordeaux wineries.

A sparkling wine to disgorge at home

Disgorgement Slovenian style

The "traditional" or "*champenoise*" method (but this term is banned on labels) for the preparation of sparkling wines causes secondary fermentation inside the bottle by the addition of sugar and yeast.

Forced to remain in the bottle, which is closed by a solid cork, the carbon dioxide generated by the fermentation process dissolves into the wine – hence the bubbles. After this second fermentation, a deposit of dead yeast falls to the bottom of the bottle – rather unattractive for a wine that is meant to embody elegance!

So champagne makers have found a solution: they store the bottles neck down and the yeast falls onto the cap. Disgorgement involves opening each bottle with a special tool, the slug of yeast coming away with each cap. As some liquid has been lost during the operation, the bottle is topped up with a little wine, perhaps a sweet one (*liqueur d'expédition*), the bottle is resealed … *et voilà*!

Manual disgorgement ("on the fly") used to be a spectacular operation. Nowadays, however, it takes place in a machine that freezes the neck of the bottle.

In Slovenia, winemaker Ales Kristančič of the Movia (Dobrovo) estate is betting that he can trust sommeliers or knowledgeable consumers to carry out this technical step and sell a wine that needs to be disgorged before drinking. "This is the only part of the process that we can outsource and which will go some way to explaining sparkling wines," says Kristančič, heir to a long line of winemakers. In the former Yugoslavia, Marshal Tito himself appreciated this winery and spared it from nationalisation, he adds.

Kristančič is also quite the comedian, as free-thinking as he seems to be self-taught, and sets the scene with coloured lights. "Watch out, always keep the bottle neck pointing downwards. We'll stick the new label on upside down, to remind people how to store our bottles."

Isn't it awkward to impose such constraints on the customer? "Not at all, sommeliers love it – adds to their value!" Rather like bartenders mixing cocktails. To help them, Kristančič provides a special key or a transparent ice bucket with a bottle opener in the base.

His *Puro* blend is original in another way too: "Unlike the traditional method, no sugar is added, nor any yeast to encourage fermentation in the bottle: only the must with its own sugar and micro-organisms, which you disgorge yourself when you open the bottle. So the wine continues to develop with its natural yeasts until it is drunk, and contains no sulphites. It has an infinite life. *Puro* is a very special sparkling wine!"

But beware: this living bottle must be kept cool. Any rise in temperature may stimulate the yeast, with explosive results.

Curious colours

Every encounter begins with a look. Examining a glass of wine (the first step at a tasting session) reveals certain characteristics that are then confirmed by nose and mouth. A deep colour often, but not always, corresponds to an intense taste: the substance of the wine is present in concentrated form. A slight disturbance in the liquid is a sign of unfiltered wine, a different kind of "substance". The green reflections in a young white wine will turn golden over the months and years. In a young red, purplish shades slowly oxidise and evolve towards orange.

Almost all colours are represented in the wine palette. *White* is rarely as clear as water; *red* ranges from carmine to deep black; *rosé* is sometimes a light red or a pale salmony tint. Strangely, the concept of colour varies from country to country.

So in France, rosé is much clearer and more orangey than elsewhere. Bordeaux claret can be anywhere between dark pink and light red. The young Portuguese white with green hues is called *vinho verde* – green wine. In the French Jura, yellow completes the range. In Italy, a cheap white wine is sold in blue bottles as the producer hopes the attractive colour of the glass will stand out on the shelves.

"Orange" wine (a white fermented with the grape skin) on the Movia estate (Slovenia)

Blanc de Blancs wines are pressed from white grapes. As most varieties of black grape give white juice, rapid pressing prevents the pigments in the skin from colouring the juice. Some winemakers are doing their best to extract white juice from varieties used exclusively for red wine – such as *Ynsolite*, a sparkling white from Cave de Tain l'Hermitage based on Syrah grapes.

Some colours, although authorised by their appellations, are certainly unusual. A still red wine (no bubbles) is produced at Bouzy in France's Champagne region. White Beaujolais is allowed but rare (Château de l'Éclair estate, Rhone valley). "White Beaujolais is as difficult to sell as a two-man coffin," a wine merchant joked.

Does the colour of a wine influence how we perceive its taste? As Baudelaire wrote, *Les parfums, les couleurs et les sons se répondent* (Perfumes, colours and sounds respond to one another). But this correspondence, known as synaesthesia, is not only a charming poetic invention, but a proven tasting fact. A tasteless and odourless red colourant added to white wine gives most wine experts the impression of red fruit. A wine sipped from a black glass won't have the same flavour as if it was in a clear glass. Colour affects the sense of taste because our brains amass different sensations and synthesise them into an overall impression.

Greek rosé from the Oenoforos estate

A rosé that defies the regulations by blending red and white grapes

What is rosé wine? A mixture of white and red? The question was raised in 2009 when certain enterprises, notably in Australia and South Africa, made the decision to combine these two colours to conquer the expanding rosé market. Led by Provence in the south of France, Old World winemakers saw red: if rosé was indeed a white with a few drops of added colour, it would taste like white, so it's not just the colour that makes the wine pink.

White wine is the juice of white grapes (or red grapes yielding white juice) pressed soon after harvest and left to ferment. Red wine, on the other hand, comes from grapes that have been macerated and fermented from one to several weeks, with their skins and seeds, before pressing. During this phase, the skins and seeds give the juice colour, flavour and tannins as the developing alcohol extracts various aromatic compounds.

The rosé technique falls between the two: red grapes with white juice macerate for several hours without fermenting, and this contact with the skins lightly colours the juice. After pressing, the coloured grape juice is fermented.

The water of grape juice (in rosé wine) or the alcohol produced by fermentation (in red wine) does not extract the same molecules.

A disturbing discovery was made at the Oenoforos estate belonging to Angelos Rouvalis, vice-president of the Greek Wine Federation: 75–85 per cent Syrah (red) and 25–15 per cent Viognier (white) on a rosé specification sheet. "The aromas of red fruit and violet come from the Syrah, those of apple, passion fruit and grapefruit from the Viognier." The taste is nothing if not expressive, somewhere between bananas and boiled sweets.

Greek palmento, Agrigento, Sicily

In theory, mixing white and red wine is banned. At Oenoforos, two colours of grape are mixed for four to eight hours and then pressed.

The juice of the two varieties is fermented at a low temperature (12 °C) for a fortnight or so.

So what the Greeks have devised is a rosé version of *Côte-rôtie*, one of the most prestigious Côtes du Rhône, which also blends Syrah with Viognier to make a full-bodied red.

White and red grape blends are rare

Blending of different coloured grapes is the exception rather than the rule. In Tuscany, the chianti regulations allow bunches of white grapes to be added to fermentation tanks to soften the reds, but the wine is still red. Bordeaux winemakers used to add some local white grapes to their claret for the same reason. In Provence, the Luberon appellation allows up to 20 per cent of the Vermentino (white) variety to be mixed with red grapes, before fermentation of course. This is not done for the colour, but because of the Vermentino aromatics.

The first wines were light in colour

Ancient Greece contributed greatly to the spread of winemaking skills by teaching the Etruscans of pre-Roman Italy, who in their turn passed their skills on to the Roman colonisers of Europe. Archaeological ruins, writings, and decorations on pottery all show that the first wines were light-coloured. The grapes crushed underfoot in a *palmento* (cistern), and the juice that was immediately stored for fermentation, could only have produced a white or a rosé. Red wine came later, when the dark skins had been left to macerate with the grape juice.

Pink champagne: a very rare exception to rosé regulations

Why does champagne come from a black grape? What is Blanc de Noirs? And red champagne?

First remarkable fact: 90 per cent of champagne bottles contain white wine, while 70 per cent of the vineyards of the Champagne region of France are planted with black grapes. Pinot Noir in particular is used for the great Burgundy reds, but also Blanc de Noirs (literally "white of blacks") by carefully avoiding colouring the pressed juice with the skins.

Wouldn't it make more sense to make a white wine from white grapes? No doubt, but Pinot Noir gives a structured framework and a delicate bouquet that is full and intense, with fine aromatic complexity: all characteristic of the great champagnes. The harvest is carried out by hand, whole bunches carefully transported in crates and quickly pressed: harvesting machines are banned as they suck in the grapes and crush them, and the skin would stain the juice. "A very light champagne shows the skill of the winemaker. For a long while, pink champagne was considered flawed, a sacrilege," asserts Hubert de Billy of Champagne Pol Roger. Blanc de Blancs designates champagnes made only from the white Chardonnay grape that covers the remaining 30 per cent of the region's vineyards.

Mumm champagne

LIAISON N°2
F
FERMÉ
CAVEAU A4
CAVEAU A3
DAUBRON
DAUBRON
LIAISON N°2 9

Automated remuage (riddling) of champagne bottles, using a machine known as a gyropalette, takes a few days (Bouvay-Ladubay, Saumur, France)

By hand, with the bottles on pupitres, a similar operation takes several weeks (Champagne Cattier, Montagne de Reims, France)

Second remarkable fact: to make their rosé (10 per cent of production), the Champagne winemakers add a little local red to the white. This mix guarantees precise colour control, an important feature for a fashionable luxury product. But isn't mixing white and red wines to make pink wine banned in theory? True, but as a second fermentation takes place in the bottles to make foam (when still wine becomes sparkling), the organoleptic characteristics of champagne aren't the same as a straightforward mix of wines of two colours.

Exception to the above facts: a few pink champagnes (1 per cent of production) come from *saigneés*, i.e. from "bleeding" the Pinot Noir skin colour into the juice). The grapes are left to macerate overnight and pressed the next day.

Thanks to public approbation, winemakers have finally seen pink champagne as a noble wine and there's even a Pol Roger rosé.

Finally, to top it all, as the law doesn't ban nuanced shades of pink, some winemakers push their luck even further, going as far as red // sparkling //champagne (a few still reds are produced in the Champagne region). In the 19th century, this curiosity was achieved by adding 25–35 per cent of red wine, followed by a red *liqueur d'expédition*. Some winemakers prepare bottles of this "very dark rosé" for home consumption, as red champagne doesn't officially exist (the trade organisation – Comité Interprofessionnel du Vin de Champagne – would expel any winemaker who dared to publicise it).

Château Bouvet-Ladubay in Touraine (Loire valley) makes a *demi-sec* (medium-dry) sparkling red called *Rubis*. Sparkling red is more widespread in Italy, especially Lambrusco and the wines of Oltrepò Pavese ("Pavia across the Po" in Lombardy), such as Bonarda.

Yellow wine

An exceptional winemaking method with astonishing results

Oenologists are strict about this: wine must be protected from oxidation as it causes a rancid taste and a stale smell, or even turns the wine to vinegar. Oxygen is life: bacteria, moulds and yeasts can't survive without it. Everybody knows that a bottle that has been opened and forgotten for a few weeks may no longer be drinkable. Oxygen is the bane of all winemakers, the reason why barrels are filled to the brim. As the wine evaporates because of the tiny amounts of oxygenation through the pores of the wood, the barrels are topped up regularly. This evaporation is poetically known as "the angels' share", and the topping up as ullage (see p. 153). Very few wines take the risk of ignoring the top-up rule. In the Jura, the local Savagnin grape yields a prized white wine. A few winemakers age it in a partially full barrel: an intriguing veil of the *Saccharomyces cerevisiae* yeast then develops on the surface.

After six years and three months, on the first weekend in February, the barrel is opened to great celebration. The wine is bottled in 0.62 litre *clavelins*. Unlike the conventional 0.75 litre bottle, this unusual measure is a tribute to "the angels' share", i.e. the liquid evaporated over the years from a litre of wine, but it seems that the *clavelin* also owes something to an English-style bottle.

Bernard Pujol, secretary of the Confrérie des Ambassadeurs des Vins Jaunes (Jura)

During its seventy-five months under a veil of yeast, the white wine takes on a bronze colour which is described as *jaune* (yellow). It looks like a sweet wine but turns out to be perfectly dry, with no residual sugars. The taste is reminiscent of walnuts, with a wonderful finish from the pronounced aromatics that have developed.

Another unusual feature is that it keeps for decades, even for hundreds of years, and an open bottle can remain for some considerable time on the shelf without unpleasant oxidation: the wine is already past that stage. The International Organisation of Vine and Wine classes it as a "speciality wine".

Note that some wineries, such as Overnoy and Puffeney, leave their *vin jaune* ageing in the barrel even longer than the six years and three months authorised by the appellation.

Other wines that "take the veil"

Spanish sherry (*xeres*) is another example of wine aged using the *sous voile* [lit. under the veil] technique.

Some winemakers in the south of France are also trying it, such as Robert and Bernard Plageoles (Gaillac) and the Jorel estate (Maury) with its *La Garrigue* wine from the rare Macabeu grape, which is aged for ten years.

Don't confuse *vin jaune* with the other Jura speciality, Macvin, made by adding marc (grape brandy distilled from the fermented mash, also known as marc) to fortify grape juice. Macvin comes in three colours: red, rosé and white.

Orange wine

Fermenting white like red, together with their skins, to make "orange wine"

Traditionally, white wine is made by pressing grapes (white or red) and fermenting the juice. For red wine it's the other way round: first ferment the grapes (red, of course) and then press them. In this way the tannins from the seeds, the colours and the aromas of the skins pass into the must, which in due course vinifies.

A few winemakers use the second method with white grapes. The resulting wine is still classified as white, but it has a deeper colour and more intense flavour and complexity, thanks to the presence of seeds and skins. It's known as "macerated white", "Italian-style" or "orange" wine – not to be confused with the drink made from orange peel soaked in white wine with added alcohol.

Slovenian winemaker Ales Kristančič makes his *Lunar* wine in this way. Destemmed Rebula grapes are piled into Burgundy barrels to macerate, skins on. Their weight bursts the skins and sets off fermentation, a process that lasts six months. The barrels are sealed, leaving an aperture that lets carbon dioxide escape. Kristančič doesn't press these grapes, he just siphons off the juice and bottles it (on the night of the full moon). Of course, this method barely yields 25 per cent of what he'd get from pressing the contents of the barrels, but the bottled wine sells at a high price. "A great wine is one that has taken a few risks," says the media-savvy winemaker, who exports 80 per cent of his production and is the winner of several international awards.

Orange wine from Giorgio Clai (Croatia)

Marie Thibault-Cabrit

In Croatia, Giorgio Clai uses the same red Burgundy method of fermentation in open barrels, although nobody from that part of France would do so with white grapes. After destemming, the grapes are macerated for thirty days and then, unlike Kristančič, Clai uses a press. "I treat red and white in the same way, along with their skins. The first year, we destemmed by hand and pressed by foot, hence the name of the wine: *Ottocento*, as in the 1800s!"

The alcohol level is high: "My white is the weakest at 15 per cent. My wines aren't afraid of food – it's rather food that's scared of them! This isn't really a wine for everyday drinking," the organic grower jokes mischievously. "I don't add sugar or yeast – I like to recognise the year and the *terroir* in the taste, which will vary depending on whether it rained or not."

In France, only a few estates make "orange wine". In Touraine, near Azay-le-Rideau, Marie Thibault-Cabrit produces her *Vino bianco* vintage from 100 per cent Sauvignon Blanc grapes that have been macerated for several months with their skins, "Italian-style", in used oak barrels. She doesn't add yeast to control the fermentation or sugar to raise the level of alcohol that the grapes would naturally yield (i.e. no chaptalisation). She doesn't use much sulphite either. In the vineyard organic treatments are used with no weedkillers, and harvesting is done by hand.

Black wine

The reputation of this wine has evolved over time, but today *black is beautiful*

A short history: there have been vineyards around Cahors in south-western France since Roman times. Barges loaded with barrels used to glide along the Lot and Garonne rivers to unload at Bordeaux, Cahors' famous rival: two colours, two regions, two styles of wine that competed for centuries.

As one of their major concerns was the conservation properties of their wine, Cahors winemakers had perfected their own methods: they dried the clusters of grapes in the sun, or heated them like prunes, and sometimes also boiled the must to concentrate the sugars. The increased volume of alcohol in the wine improved conservation. Vintages from the slopes around Cahors, Gaillac and Bergerac were exported to England and Russia.

This method also had the effect of concentrating and darkening the wine. The local Malbec grape could in any case yield a wine as black as ink, but unfortunately very tannic and with a rough, rustic character – like tea that's been brewed too long.

In contrast, under their more temperate Atlantic climate the Bordeaux winemakers pressed black and white varieties together to soften the blend.

English customers came to differentiate the stylish Bordeaux "claret" from the "black wine" of Cahors. So the "black", with its longer shelf-life, competed with Bordeaux wines against a backdrop of territorial disputes between the kings of England and France. In response to such threats, the Bordeaux winemakers managed to negotiate and keep a certain privilege: transporting wine from the Cahors region to Bordeaux was banned until Christmas, which gave the locals time to ship out that year's vintage. New wine was the best in those days, so it had to be sold quickly. For some five hundred years this "Bordeaux privilege" consolidated the power of the best-known appellation in the world.

The Bordeaux winemakers, however, had no hesitation in mixing their paler wines with some from Cahors to strengthen the colour and alcohol content. This practice led to local names from the Cahors region gradually being forgotten in favour of Bordeaux wines, especially since the epithet *Carte noire* applied to a cheap blend of Cahors gave the "black wine" a poor reputation.

The dark brew made a comeback in Argentina in the late 19th century. Frenchman Michel Pouget introduced Malbec to the country, which now grows 39,000 hectares (compared with only 4,000 hectares in France). The Malbec variety has become emblematic in South America, gaining such a reputation that Cahors winemakers now use the term "French Malbec". The winemaking style does differ though – New World Malbec has a few grams of residual sugar, while its French cousin is completely dry.

Extraordinary ageing methods

To store and transport food, prehistoric peoples first used animal paunches and lightweight goatskins. As they became sedentary cultivators, they began to make pottery and clay amphorae, and to split tree trunks into planks to assemble waterproof barrels, a real feat of Celtic precision. The barrel became the winemakers' emblem.

The Gauls didn't make their own wine before the Gallo-Roman era, so the wealthier among them would acquire a Roman amphora of wine in exchange for a slave. Producers and navigators realised that in order to preserve their wine and export it to lucrative destinations, they had to seal the amphorae with a wooden or cloth stopper, or seal it with pitch or resin. So for thousands of years the best wine was new wine, from the latest harvest. From the previous year there was only a memory and a jug of vinegar.

An inexplicable phenomenon sometimes occurred. The precious liquid, whether stored in barrel or amphora, would deteriorate or on the contrary it would improve, the hardness disappearing. Magic? Before the discoveries of Pasteur (1822–1895) about the life of micro-organisms, fermentation and conservation remained a mystery.

Today we know that the oak cask plays a triple role: first, it stores the wine; second, it transfers tannins and a woody taste that is more or less roasted (depending to what extent the planks or staves have been heated); and, third, it allows a tiny dose of oxygen to pass through the pores of the wood. This micro-oxygenation changes the wine flavours to more flexible, rounded tannins that are less hard.

The woody, toasty taste comes from the heat used to bend the planks in barrel-making. This characteristic taste transferred to the wine is loved and hated in about equal measure. A number of tasters in fact believe that ageing in wooden barrels standardises a wine and neutralises the effect of its *terroir* and grape variety.

"If you want to disguise a wine, wood is perfect. Even with rather watery grapes, it adds a certain thickness, like large wheels on a car with a small engine," quips winemaker Frank Cornelissen from Mount Etna (Sicily).

Young barrels, aged between one and three years, do give wine an aroma and some flattering flavours. Some cheap wines with a woody taste have even had oak chips or granules soaked in them: instead of putting wine into the wood, wood is put into the wine.

Other winemakers, such as Fritz Wieninger from Vienna, temper these remarks: "Like pepper in cooking, oak is a spice. I use it for my Chardonnay, but with care, because it reduces the fruitiness. I like the wine to reveal the *terroir* of its region."

The wood for a barrel will have been heated to a greater or lesser degree. The woodiness will be stronger in a new barrel and less after at least two or three harvests. The size of the barrel also plays a part in the amount of impregnation: ageing in large casks adds an almost imperceptible woodiness but welcome micro-oxygenation.

Finally, although almost all barrels are made from oak, some winemakers choose other trees, such as brothers Alex and Uros Klinec from Slovenia: "Our red is aged in cherry or oak barrels, the white in acacia or mulberry. Acacia gives a honeyed taste, exotic and floral; mulberry is fruity." Acacia, cherry and mulberry don't have the typical oak tannins. But their use is not new, as the oenology and wine-producing magazine *La Bourgogne* recorded in 1861: "For white wine, mulberry and acacia seem better suited than oak."

Wood is expensive and difficult to clean. So other materials are used to manufacture the tanks in which wine is fermented and stored: concrete, stainless steel, PVC plastic, glass, fibreglass, clay ... Each has specific qualities: the high thermal inertia of concrete maintains a stable temperature; steel, on the other hand, cools or warms easily, which is convenient for controlling the winemaking temperature.

Concrete or wood tanks must be filled to the brim, without air, like a topped-up bottle, otherwise the wine could suffer. However, steel tanks can be partially filled and the wine protected by an airtight sliding cover system and inflatable air chamber, which is handy for storing varying volumes.

Some plastics, however, leach phthalates and bisphenol (chemicals harmful to health) into the wine.

Other unusual containers: egg-shaped concrete tanks; amphorae, which despite being porous, fragile and difficult to clean are back in fashion; or barrels with a transparent cover, used for educational purposes – to show the development of *vin jaune*, for example (see photo p. 214).

There are other unusual methods of conditioning wine: Maury is stored in glass carboys, outside, open and exposed to the elements (see p. 231); the Saint-Pourçain estate in the Auvergne region of central France ages its *Lo Mountogno*, both red and white, for two years 1,100 metres up in the Cantal mountains; while other producers store their wine underwater, either in rivers or the sea ...

The world's largest wooden barrel can be found at Caves Byrrh, in Thuir (Pyrénées-Orientales, south of France). It holds 1 million litres.

Three types of container: concrete, wood and stainless steel
(Château de la Crée, Burgundy)

Underwater wine

What happens when bottles or tanks are submerged?

In 2010, a ship loaded with bottles of Veuve Clicquot Ponsardin, Heidsieck & Co and Juglar champagnes was found 170 years after sinking in the Baltic Sea. These bottles, survivors of the shipwreck, were soon snapped up at auction. Are they drinkable? How does the wine react to the special conditions of the watery depths? The low temperature slows biological changes, whereas the currents that disturb the bottles accelerate changes.

Several experiments have studied the effect of the marine environment: the Drappier champagne house left 660 bottles of *Brut nature* and *Grande Sendrée 2005* for a year in the Gulf of Saint-Malo, at a temperature of 9 °C and 17 metres down in the darkness. In 2009, the Slovenian cooperative Goriška Brda also immersed crates of bottles in a freshwater stream for several years (www.klet-brda.si). Yannick Heude, wine merchant and president of the "Immersion" association, studies the evolution of wines in the marine environment: "Immersed champagne turns a darker, yellower colour, with a less lively effervescence, which would seem to support the idea that the ageing process is speeded up."

In the bay of Saint-Jean-de-Luz (south-west France), winemaker Emmanuel Poirmeur will try anything when experimenting with ageing wine: he ferments it in submerged plastic vats, with the involvement of Basque fishermen: "What interests me is the behaviour of yeast in these conditions. In the old days, winemakers took account of the weather and the atmospheric pressure, which can vary by a factor of ten underwater, because of the tides. The temperature is 10–13 °C in winter, 17 °C in summer. So I use the ocean as an energy resource that supplies the temperature, thermal inertia, movement and counter-pressure required to make sparkling wines that it would be impossible for me to recreate ashore. I patented the method in 2007 and someone is writing a thesis on it at Montpellier University.

I'd like to pay tribute to a pioneer in this field, Jean-Louis Saget, who left some bottles of wine in oyster beds in the 1990s." So Poirmeur prepares 500-litre leak-proof, gas-porous "Flextanks" in polyethylene, to which he adds sugar and yeast, as in a second fermentation of champagne. Divers tow them out and attach them underwater. He is making two wines, one 100 per cent maritime and the other blended with 10 per cent of the underwater wine: "10 per cent, that's enough to change the flavours. I blend, just as with barrels. I notice that the wines are fruitier, with notes of lemon, lime and yuzu."

Ancient wines

Which are the oldest wines in the world?
What do they taste like?

Dedicated collectors are sometimes willing to pay tens of thousands of euros for historic bottles that have miraculously survived, a fragile testimony to the work of winemakers from other centuries.

One of the most expensive, a 1787 Château Lafitte engraved with the initials of Thomas Jefferson, third president of the United States, was valued at €125,000.

The oldest isn't necessarily the most expensive: a bottle of 1947 Château Cheval-Blanc (considered the best year of the last century), accompanied by a document detailing its history and origins, broke the record at €223,967.

Other safe havens for ancient wines:

The Massandra winery in the Crimea is thought to have a collection of over a million bottles, including a 1775 sherry. The cellars escaped the Russian Revolution of 1917 and the Nazi invasion of the Second World War.

The Hospices de Strasbourg have a barrel containing a wine dated 1472. General Leclerc would have been entitled to a glass when he liberated the city in 1944. Of course, as the barrel will have been topped up to offset natural evaporation through the wood, there may no longer be much trace of medieval grapes.

*Vin de paille (straw wine) at auction during the Percée du Vin Jaune festival
(Jura, France)*

Achaia Clauss (Patras, Greece)

Although excavations of ancient sites have revealed many dried-out wine residues, the oldest find in liquid form was in the tomb of a Roman legionnaire dating from the years 325 to 350. The Historical Museum of the Palatinate in Speyer (Germany) displays this curiosity in its Wine Museum section. However, as the bottle hasn't been opened, the type of liquid remains can only be guessed at. The museum also has a 1687 bottle from the Steinauer vineyard, near Naumburg in Saxony.

www.museum.speyer.de

Few collectors open these extremely old bottles: it's too much of a risk to expose them as undrinkable, losing an investment along with a dream. One of the most reputable wine collections in the world is that of Michel Chasseuil, author of *Les 100 bouteilles extraordinaires de la plus belle cave du monde*. He never opens any of them.

In his own cellar, François Audouze keeps over 40,000 exceptional bottles. He organises "wine-dinners" through his Académie des Vins Anciens – because he does drink them. He's even developed a "simple way to revive wines that may still be drinkable: open the bottle carefully four hours before drinking. Whatever you do, don't touch it or decant it. Serve it four hours later. That's all." Some bottles have aged badly, others are extraordinary, but all evoke strong emotions. On his blog, Audouze records his tasting experiences in precise and sensitive terms: "The oldest wine I've tasted dated from 1690, but it was nothing special. But what a treat to drink a wine made under Louis XIV! The oldest delicious wine I ever drank was from 1727. A piece of eternity."

www.academiedesvinsanciens.com

Tasting several bottles from the same estate, going back in time, is known as *grande verticale* in French. It reveals the characteristics of the *terroir* and how they were expressed in the climatic conditions of each year. In his cellar (excavated under the vineyard in 1540), a winemaker from south of the Sarthe (north-western France), who insists on remaining anonymous, recently opened his ancient family wines in the presence of expert Jacques Puisais.

All were from the Loir river *terroir* that has become the *Jasnières* appellation. The winemaker started with the more recent vintages, taking samples from the barrel with a pipette, and continued with bottles covered in limestone dust: 1985, 1976, 1959, 1947, 1934, 1921, 1903, 1893, 1834, 1796, "and even a bottle of 1783 that bore up magnificently, offering – after it had been open for two hours – the aroma of spice and cloves, and the taste of burnt plums, game birds, seaweed and parsnip roots".

It's an emotional experience to taste a wine that unknown people have harvested, vinified and kept for eight generations. It's like going back in time: "The *Jasnières* Chenin Blanc grape, turning to amber mahogany after a century or two, expresses a complexity of aromas of gingerbread, orange peel, white pepper, cedar or sometimes muscat, old Armagnac, candied fruit, truffles …". In the plant kingdom, only wine, whether outstanding or past its best, lets you experience the flavour of past times. These ancient wines are drinkable – barring accidents – and sometimes they are sublime.

And the laurels for the longest dynasty of winemakers go to the Italian Antinori family: twenty-six generations since 1385.

www.antinori.it

Striking packaging

"It's not the bottle that counts but the contents …"
Alfred de Musset, La coupe et les lèvres

For thousands of years wine was sold in bulk rather than by the bottle: people brought their containers to be filled from the last harvest's barrel or jars kept in the cool of the cellar.

In the streets of Florence you can still see little window hatches known as *buchette del vino* ("wine holes") low down in the walls of some palazzos. In former times the owners cultivated their own vines and sold their wine at these counters, in which customers placed their coins and empty pitchers (see *Secret Florence* in this series of guidebooks).

Today, many Italian cooperatives still distribute wine with pumps that wouldn't be out of place in a service station, and customers bring their containers along to be filled up.

Some bars, such as the Baron Rouge in Paris, also sell wine directly from vats. It has to be drunk quickly or bottled to avoid spoiling by oxidation.

The region around Vienna (Austria) has kept a wonderful link with the past: over 800 hectares of vineyards cultivated by 300 growers, half of whom run their own *Heuriger*, a tavern where they serve only young wines from the previous year's harvest (*Heuer* means "this year"). These *Heuriger* are so popular that in the city's wine-producing districts other cafés and bars can't compete with them. You don't go to the bar, but to the local winery. Their signposting is rudimentary – if a pine branch is hung over the entrance, the tavern is open. And you'll often be served not by professional waiters but by the vineyard workers themselves.

From barrel to bottle: Rocaudy's mini bottling plant in Languedoc (France)

"I like the fact that the person who serves the wine has helped make it, that they feel the power of nature," asserts Rainer Christ, who runs a 20-hectare vineyard. "Our *Heuriger* is open six months a year and the rest of the time we work the land. Pensioners come along in the afternoons, young people in the evenings." Despite their success, the *Heuriger* have kept things simple: *Grüner Veltliner* (Green Veltliner), from Austria's iconic grape, starts at €1 a glass.

This tradition is firmly rooted in Vienna. In 1784, Emperor Joseph II allowed families who owned vineyards to keep a tavern. Ever since, they've cultivated the land around their cellars and sold their wines directly to the public, accompanied by homemade food sold by weight. These direct-selling enthusiasts take a few liberties that other winemakers might not, such as serving grape juice to children or teetotallers, and preparing *glühwein* (spiced hot wine) in winter, perhaps outside in a snowy vineyard. In summer, they dilute their ordinary wine with soda. This low-alcohol mixture known as spritzer (not to be confused with the *spritz* aperitif of northern Italy) is refreshing and ubiquitous. "I don't like watering down my wine, says Fritz Wieninger, but that's how it's done in Vienna in the summer. It's much nicer than beer. Of course I also make gourmet wine."

The *Kellergasse* ("streets of cellars" or "villages with no chimneys") are characteristic of the outlying districts of Vienna. The city hall, which owns a third of the vineyards, has classed them all as land that cannot be built on. Tens of thousands of Viennese jog, walk or cycle through the vineyards, before a breakfast drink and snack in the *Heuriger*, which are also accessible by bus or tram.

Although glass bottles were already being manufactured by the ancient Greeks, the artisanal process meant that they were in short supply. It was only with 20th-century industrialisation that bottles became all-important for storing small quantities of wine.

Glass, although completely recyclable, has to be melted down and is heavy to transport.

A new type of container, the bag-in-box (BiB), or simply "boxed wine", has appeared on the market in the last few years. This packaging consists of a plastic bag inside a cardboard box. Light and economical, it doesn't let in air as the bag empties and the wine will keep for several weeks after opening. In France, boxed wine already accounts for nearly half the volume of wine sold in cafés, hotels and restaurants, with the current trend for "wine by the glass", as well as in the shops. These wine boxes aren't to be confused with the catastrophic *cubitainer* (rigid plastic cube) which on opening let in the air and oxidised the wine.

Odd bottles

Why so many different types of bottle?
What other original containers are there?

The traditional chianti flask from Tuscany, a relic of the days when wine bottles were individually made by a glassblower, is covered with braided straw or wicker to protect it.

Glassmakers began to manufacture tall, cylindrical bottles that would hold more wine. Four traditional designs were adopted around the world: Burgundy (near enough to the original curved shape), Champagne (a chunky reinforced version), Rhine (tall and tapered) and Bordeaux (high-shouldered).

There is a logic behind the differences in shape: the heavy champagne bottle retains the pressure; the Bordeaux "shoulders" capture any sediment in the tannic red wines on pouring; and the elegant Rhine bottle, designed for white or light red wine with no sediment, doesn't need the shoulders. In the gloom of the cellar, a bottle could be identified by touch. On the shelves at the shop, these four shapes help the public to visually identify a wine-producing region and a particular type of wine.

Despite this typology, the shape of bottles is fairly unrestricted. Any appellation or wine producer can celebrate an event or a new vintage with a special design, a moulding in relief or coloured glass, with the aim of intriguing and capturing the attention of the consumer.

Italian bottles are often distinguished by their original forms and lively colours. Such a plethora of initiatives reflects the importance of local heritage and the creativity of designers working with a network of industrial and regional glassmakers who are used to delivering small orders.

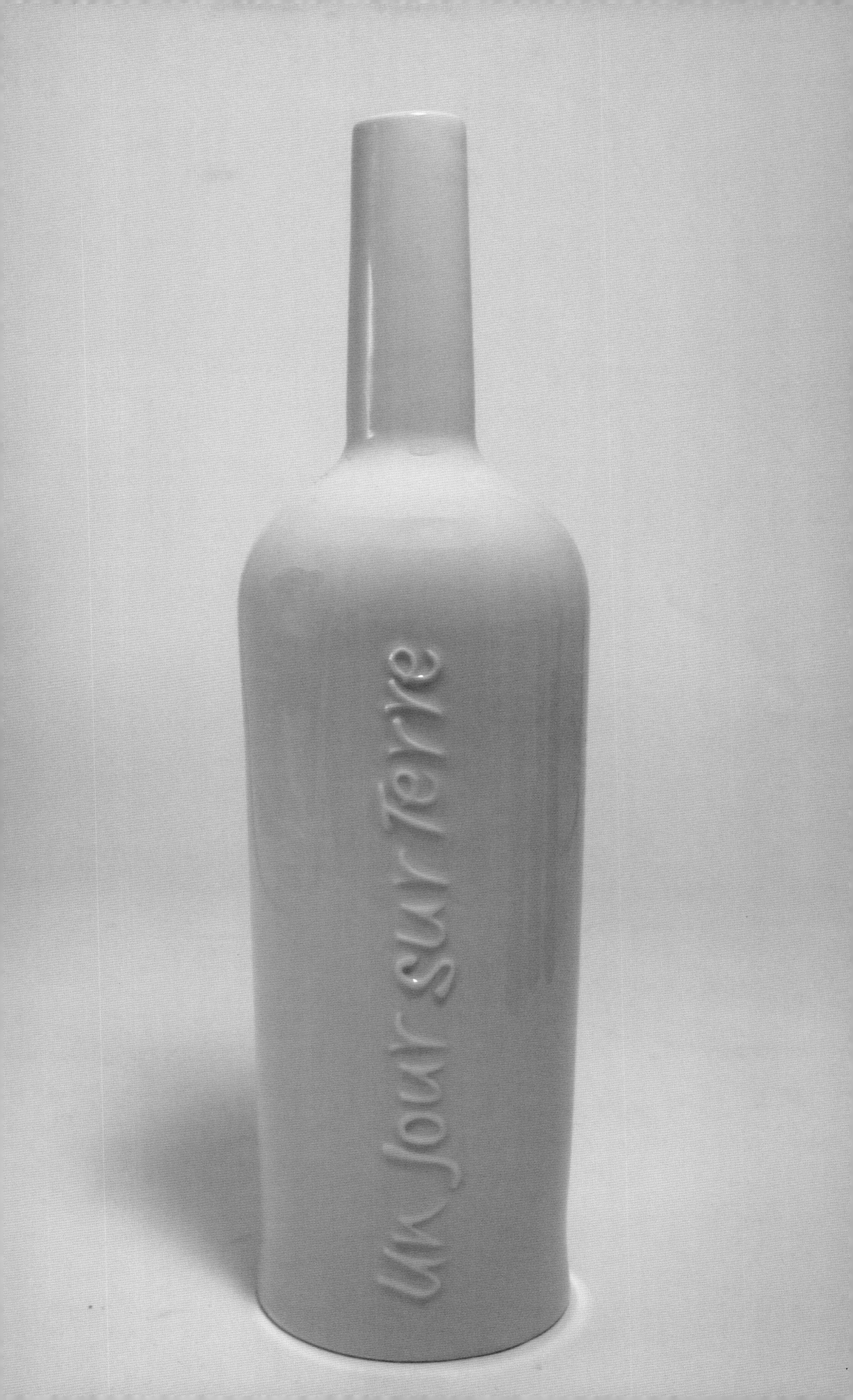
Un Jour Sur Terre

Aldo Franco, for example, a packaging designer from Verona (Italy), defines himself as an "architect of glass, because such work on shape has its technical, industrial and aesthetic aspects". He revived the *Albeisa* or Alba bottle for wines from that region of Piedmont. "The standard bottle is intended for the mass market, while the more original ones are for niche markets, restaurants and bars, or for export."

An original bottle design distinguishes the wine in the public eye and gets it noticed, as the heavy bottles of some Chinese wines and champagne highlight the value of the product. Another advantage is that moulding the AOC logo in the glass reduces fraud as the bottles are more difficult to copy.

There are a number of disadvantages to non-standard bottles, however. Designing a new shape and making a mould is expensive in engineering, worker and machine time.

Eco-design, which favours lightweight yet strong bottles to save on glass and transport costs, is a vast challenge to the industry. Unconventional bottles slow down bottling lines and complicate packaging, transport and storage. Last but not least, consumers, who already have to cope with the large number of appellations, grape varieties and brands, could be confused.

Some examples among the most unusual creations:

Porcelain at the Azémar estate at Saint-Maurice-sur-Eygues in the Rhône valley (see p. 243). Véronique and Stéphane Azémar make their organic *Un jour sur terre* Cahors in amphorae and sell it in porcelain bottles.

So their wine is "from the earth, aged in earth and bottled in earth". The other curiosity of the village is a barrel dating from the 13th century, encircled by staves of wood.

The golden bottle of *Armand de Brignac* champagne, the rappers' mythical blend, as Jay Z revealed in one of his clips. It's an amusing story: the rapper, who usually stuck to the *Cristal de Roederer* vintage, heard an interview with the DG of Roederer champagnes deploring the association between his brand and rap. Annoyed, Jay Z called for a boycott of Roederer and transferred his affections to *Armand de Brignac* at €300 to €400 a bottle. In late 2014 he even took over the distribution of his favourite brand under the ace of spades logo.

Note that not only is the opaque gold-plating a distinctive marketing tool but it protects the wine from light and preserves the flavour.

Armand de Brignac isn't the most expensive champagne in the world, however, as golden bottles set with diamonds regularly break records at auction. Jean-Jacques Cattier, producer of *Armand de Brignac*, puts this in perspective: "Our goal isn't to beat records. We can fix a solid gold wire-cap to the bottle, or anything else unconventional, and say it's the most expensive in the world. Another producer will add a few more carats and the bottle will be even more expensive. We're only talking about the odd item or a few dozen bottles."

The Jura clavelin

Specially designed for *vin jaune* (see p. 212), the significance of the 62 centilitre bottle is that only 62 cl remains from each litre after the 75-month maturation period of a "yellow wine". The missing 38 cl is the famous "angels' share".

Original stoppers

The cork prevents contact with oxygen in the air, which would turn wine to vinegar. The ancient Greeks and Romans understood the need to seal their amphorae of wine with cork or a greasy substance.

Although cork is often still used, it sometimes causes a "cork taint" that can be avoided by using synthetic materials. Some modern stoppers make the most of their plastic origins and flaunt bright colours adapted to the bottle design and label. Others just mimic the traditional cork.

The screw cap, dear to Anglo-Saxons, is convenient because it doesn't need a corkscrew and can be readily opened and closed, even if the popping sound is no longer an option.

Pascal Verheaghe, winemaker at Château du Cèdre (Cahors), has this to say: "By choosing screw caps, sales increase in some countries such as Australia and in others, such as Belgium, they fall." The Americans love them, the Russians hate them. Tests show that a quality wine can age equally well in a bottle with a metal cap and one with a traditional cork.

The most original stopper comes from Austrian winemaker Fritz Wieninger. For this purist, "Traditional corks are either too expensive or poor quality, synthetic corks are out of the question and screw caps look rather cheap." He has chosen a glass stopper sealed with a silicone ring (see photo opposite).

Finally, in the style of the magnums produced by Daniel Le Conte des Floris (Languedoc-Roussillon), some winemakers dip the bottle necks in melted wax to create a handsome old-style product, something artisanal and of value. The wax also stops any infiltration of air.

Vinolok glass stoppers from Comptoir de la Cave (Perpignan, France)

Labels with a difference

How can a label express the character of a wine?

Followers of wine labels, known as *buveurs d'étiquettes* ("label drinkers"), are particularly fond of the prestige of a famous name or a vintage year. The wine label and name play a part in the tasting sensation. The eye, like the palate, influences the brain.

Bordeaux châteaux and Burgundy grand crus don't need novelty labels: on the contrary. A view of the estate in red and black, some classic typography, and a pledge of good taste and continuity of tradition, all reassure the customer.

For lesser-known appellations, the graphic design encapsulates typical features of the contents, such as floral notes or fizz.

Like writers, winemakers are the authors of their wines, signing them with their own names. The name of the wine is similar to a book title, and the name of the appellation – announcing a style, a family of wines – might be compared to a book publisher.

As manufacturing special bottles for different wines would be considerably more expensive, the label is where creativity – especially in the graphics – comes into its own. Here are a few examples among countless others:

Some winemakers name their wines after their children or in tribute to a beloved ancestor: a story to tell, and a potential gift for someone who bears that name too. Others resolutely choose puns and provocation: *On s'en bat les couilles* (we don't give a shit), *Boire tue* (drinking kills), *Vin de merde* (crap wine) and *Vin de bagnole* (old jalopy wine) are all excellent, unpretentious wines that aim to attract attention with an irreverent name and design. Despite the casual tone, their savvy marketing approach avoids any potentially divisive topics such as religion and politics.

With very few exceptions, the vintage (which is generally marked on the label) follows the Western Gregorian calendar, the Hebrew or Jewish calendar for kosher wine, or the Buddhist calendar in Monsoon valley (Thailand). *Vin de table*, which is often a blend from different years, has no authorisation to display a vintage. Some rebellious producers of "table wine" refuse to obey appellation rules and sell by reputation alone under their name and that of the estate, although indicating the vintage on the label as a lot number, such as L-014 for 2014.

A personalised bottle celebrates an event, perhaps a wedding. Taiwan winemakers make speciality bottles for all life's occasions: graduations, military service, a new job …

Numerous websites suggest printing your own label, which of course helps them sell wine at the same time …

The Mabouteille.fr website offers customised wooden crates, cutting boards, coasters and door escutcheons …

ItsMyWine.com goes further, offering users the chance to mix their own blend from fifteen grape varieties selected by Olivier Magny and Nicolas Paradis, founder of the Parisian wine bar O Château. A genuine "made-to-measure wine" is delivered with customised labels and crates.

Illegal labels hijack or copy names. For example, only Hungary benefits from the Tokaj appellation (Tokay in English), whereas the Italians and Slovenes have historically cultivated the Tocai grape. So they rant against the obligation to call their variety Sauvignonasse or Sauvignon Vert and label it Tocai Friulano, disputing the differences between Tocai and Tokaj.

Deluxe labels: Monte Rossa chooses expensive embossed-metal plates, to the most beautiful effect, for its top-of-the-range sparkling *Cabochon* vintage from the Franciacorta appellation (Lombardy, Italy).

Wooden labels

Why is *Le Faîte* sold with a pinewood label attached to a wax medallion?

For their best bottles, the ones they want to hand on to their descendants, Gascon winemakers had no faith in paper labels that could easily become damaged and unreadable. So after hermetically sealing the stopper with wax, they wired a carved wooden label to the neck, bearing the name and vintage of the wine. The bottles were then buried in sand or clay, at a more stable temperature than in a cellar. Old bottles with wooden labels were attached to AOC application files to demonstrate the antiquity of this practice.

Today, in its honour, Plaimont Producteurs (www.plaimont.com) make two special blends called *Le Faîte*, using three grape varieties for each: Tannat, Pinenc and Cabernet Sauvignon for red; Arrufiac, Gros Manseng and Petit Courbu for white. These characteristic local varieties (with the exception of Cabernet Sauvignon) are blended with the assistance of a wine expert, often one of the best in the world. A limited edition of a few thousand bottles is sealed with wax – red for red wine, yellow for white – and fitted with a label made from *pin des Landes* (maritime pine), which gives the mandatory legal information (name, year, strength, volume, warning for pregnant women). A wax medallion embossed with the Plaimont name attaches the label's brass wire to the bottle. This full-bodied, up-market wine is aimed at wine merchants, fine grocery stores and gourmet restaurants.

With a nod to the tradition of burying the bottles, the wooden label also highlights the importance of the subsoil in grape development: in south-west France where Plaimont is based, the clay and limestone around Plaisance are said to give the wines power and help them age well; the sandy soils of Aignan add finesse and elegance; the district around the village of Saint-Mont, with its clay soil and pebbles, brings strength, density and character.

Wines index

12 UVE (Italy) 110

Chemin de bois (France) 191

Armand de Brignac (France) . . . 244

Asti spumante (Italy) 157

Banyuls (France) 172

Beaujolais blanc (France) . . . 201

Biscoitos (Portugal) 59

Black wine (France) 220

Bonarda (Italy) 211

Bourgogne Passe-Tout-Grains (France) . 98

C de Centeilles (France) 99

Cabochon (Italy) 251

Cerdon du Bugey (France) . . . 157

Champagne rosé (France) . . . 208

Champagne rouge (France) . . . 211

Château Blissa (France) 192

Château Charonne (France) . . . 47

Château Coquillas (France) . . . 48

Chianti (Italy) 242

Cilaos (Réunion) 23

Clos des amandiers (Georgia) . . 183

Côte-rôtie (France) 207

Cristal (France) 244

Donnas (Italy) 23

Drappier Grande Sendrée (France) . 228

Enfer d'Arvier (Italy) 23

Flauto (Italy) 110

Fragola (Italy) 95

Garhiofilatum (France) 170

Gemischter Satz (Austria) 98

Goutte d'Or (France) 44

Grüner Veltliner (Austria) . . . 240

Guinguet (France) 44

Hermitage blanc (France) . . . 173

Hypocras (France) 170

Ice wine (Canada) 36

Ice wine (Taiwan) 28

Jasnières (France) 237

Crimea Kagor (Russian Federation) . 172

La Garrigue (France) 215

La Salle (Italy) 23

Lajido (Portugal) 59

Lambrusco (Italy) 211

Le Clos Montmartre (France) . . . 46

Le Faîte (France) 252

Limoux méthode ancestrale (France) . 157

Lo Mountogno (France) 227

Lunar (Slovenia) 216

Macvin (France) 215

Madeira (Portugal) 172

Mateus (Portugal) 164

Maury (France) 172

Metodo classico (Italy) 130

Mille e uno (Italy) 160

Mon cœur (France) 173

Monsoon Valley (Thailand) . . . 251

Morgex (Italy) 23

Moscato di noto (Italy) 173

Muro Sant'Angelo (Italy) 160

Night orient (France) 159

Noval nacional (Portugal) 143

Nuage (France) 157

Oenoforos (Greece) 204

Orange wine (Slovenia) 216

Orto (Italy) 67

Ottocento (Croatia) 219

Our Wine (Georgia) 183

Pacherenc de la Saint-Sylvestre (France) 120

Pacherenc du Vic-Bilh (France) . . . 120

Passito di Pantelleria (Italy) 116

Passito liquoroso (Italy) 172

Paule Courtil (France) 99

Pineau des Charentes (France/Quebec) 27

Plume (France) 159

Pol Roger (France) 211

Port (Portugal) 172

Pure Carménère (France) 77

Puro (Slovenia) 199

Quattuor (France) 91

Rasteau doré (France) 172

Rasteau rouge (France) 172

Rou Ding Xiang (China) 35

Rubis (France) 211

Ruffus (Belgium) 191

Sangue d'oro (Italy) 119

Sangue di Giuda (Italy) 173

Savoie (France) 20

Sherry (Spain) 215

Sinefinis (Slovenia/Italy) 86

Straw wine (France) 172

Suntime Yili River (China) 35

Superprimitivo (Italy) 160

Sushi Time (China) 35

Terrantez (Portugal) 59

Tokaji Aszú (Hungary) 119

Two Islands (Indonesia) 27

Un jour sur terre (France) 244

Verdelho (Portugal) 58

Verdelho des Açores (Portugal) . . . 59

Versoaln (Italy) 143

Vieilles vignes françaises (France) . . . 57

Vignes pré-phylloxériques France) . . . 57

Villa dei misteri (Italy) 63

Vin de glace (Canada) 36

Vin de glace (Taiwan) 28

Vin de paille du Jura (France) 172

Vin de Suresnes (France) 47

Vin jaune (France) 212

Vinho verde (Portugal) 200

Vino bianco (France) 219

Vino della pace (Italy) 82

Xeres (Spain) 215

Yacochuya (Argentine) 23

Yellow wine (France) 212

Ynsolite (France) 202

Acknowledgements

Angélica Oury and her family, Frédéric Beaugendre, Marie-Claude Fondanaux, Thierry Joly, Patrick Poivre d'Arvor, Michèle Piron, Brigitte Viennot and Véronique Magnoni (Vinconnexion), Diane Caillard (Plaimont Producteurs), Bruno Quenioux (Philovino), Laurent Courtial et Caroline Campalto (Rouge Granit), Diane Galland, Adeline Chazelle-Pinot and Sophie Cartier-Bresson (Vivactis), Sophie Pallas (Autrement Vins), Youlia Baptiste and Victorine Crispel de Beler (Pain et Vin Compagnie), Pierrick Pichot and Janine Marmorat (Open2Europe), Flavio Mascia (restaurant Fontanarosa), Bertrand Collard (La Vigne), Marion Ivaldi (Vitisphère), Walter Eberenz (Der Badische Winzer), Prince Francesco Spadafora, Anna-Maria Terenghi, Andrea Terenghi and Ferdinando Calaciura (GranVia, Palermo), Emmanuelle Smadja (Alchimie), André Deyrieux (Winetourisminfrance), Pierre Guigui (Amphore), Anne Lefèvre, Federica Galbesi (Enit), Joseph Antonacci (Ice), Élisabeth de Meurville (Guide des Gourmands), Corinne Boulbès (Oenovideo), Michel Dovaz, Léna Lherbier, Jean-Bernard Métais, Ann Bouard, Grégory Michel, Egmont Labadie, Christine Ontivero, Hélène Piot, Alain Ségelle, Jean-Emmanuel Simon, Pierre Kergall, Cindy Helier, Jérome Gagnez and Nicolas Valluet.

Photo credits

Pierrick Bourgault: 4, 6, 9, 12, 14, 17, 18, 21, 22, 29, 30, 31, 33, 34, 41, 45, 46, 47, 51, 52, 53, 55, 56, 61, 62, 70, 72, 75, 76, 77, 79, 80, 87, 90, 93, 94, 97, 99, 106, 108, 117, 118, 119, 121, 122, 123, 125, 127, 128, 129, 131, 132, 133, 135, 136, 141, 142, 150, 153, 161, 162, 163, 165, 166, 168, 169, 171, 175, 176, 178, 179, 181, 182, 183, 185, 186, 189, 190, 197, 198, 201, 205, 206, 209, 210, 213, 217, 219, 221, 226, 229, 233, 234, 236, 239, 241, 249, 250
An Autumn Idyll by Francis Davis Millet (1892) – Brooklyn Museum: 3 – Sylvie Belanger (L'Orpailleur): 11 – Hong Ji-Bei: 19 – Hatten: 25, 26 – Grégory Michel: 33 – Luc Villeneuve (L'Orpailleur): 37, 38 – Thierry Joly: 42, 59 – Vinconnexion: 49 – G. Bombieri: 65, 66, 67 – *Automne* by John William Godward (1900), private collection: 69 – Cormons: 83, 84, 85 – *Treille*, by Friedrich Kersting (1815) – Kunst Museum Düsseldorf: 89 – *Vendanges sur hautains géants au XVIIIe siècle* by Jacob Philipp Hackert: 105 – Christelle Espinasse (La Colombette): 101, 102 – Piwi International: 103 – Paradiso: 111, 114, 115 – Michel Loriot: 112 – Grotta del Sole: 145, 146 – Quintessence: 149, 193, 194 – V. Bernard (Syndicat des Vins du Bugey): 155 – Thierry Navarre: 156 – Christophe Henry: 172 – Marie Angliviel (Lettres de Châteaux): 202, 203 – Philippe Bruniaux (Vins du Jura): 214 – Marie Thibault-Cabrit: 218 – Mathieu Drouet/Take a Sip: 223 – C. Goussard (Mas Amiel): 224 – Champagne Drappier: 230, 231 – Domaine Azémar: 243 – Vinolok: 247 – Plaimont Producteurs: 253

Design: **Stéphanie Benoit**
Translation: **Caroline Lawrence**
Proofreading: **Jana Gough**

© JONGLEZ 2016
Registration of copyright: February 2016 – Edition: 01
ISBN: 978-2-36195-139-9
Printed in China by Toppan Leefung Pte. Ltd